# MY WATERY SELF

*Memoirs of a Marine Scientist*

# MY WATERY SELF

*Memoirs of a Marine Scientist*

STEPHEN SPOTTE

THREE ROOMS PRESS
NEW YORK

*My Watery Self: Memoirs of a Marine Biologist*
by Stephen Spotte



ISBN: 978-1-941110-16-4
Library of Congress Control Number: 2014951135

Cover and interior design:
KG Design International
www.katgeorges.com

Three Rooms Press
New York, NY
www.threeroomspress.com

Distributed by:
PGW/Perseus
www.pgw.com

*To tell you the truth, I'm only happy when I'm my watery self. When I fall asleep in that state, I'm spared the trouble of dreaming. For water has no past.*

Mia Couto
*Under the Frangipani*

## CONTENTS

# MY WATERY SELF

# *Introduction*

STEPHEN SPOTTE, PHD, PROBABLY BEST considered a marine scientist, can certainly be portrayed as a renaissance man extraordinaire. He continues to perform brilliantly in many different fields. As Ella Fitzgerald sang, "Things may come, and things may go, but this is one thing you ought to know: T'aint what you do it's the way that you do it." Perhaps he should be characterized by his questioning of why and how. For those readers who know Steve or his scientific works and would like to know more about him, *My Watery Self* is that opportunity.

Most of his many accomplishments, both peer-reviewed and popular scientific as well as fictional, are published prolifically in a variety of sole-authored books. Lists occur at the end of this introduction. All are well written and packed with material useful for presenting lectures. I know, because I included much of his explained information for maintaining fishes and invertebrates in both his early (1970, 1973) and later (1992) tomes in some of my own lectures and research. His complete taxonomic, biological, and public health presentation on the many species of small South American catfishes, some of which enter the urethras of people while urinating in the streams, makes for memorable discussion on vertebrate "parasites" of humans. Whatever he writes about, he sneaks in a wonderful phrase to explain any feature.

In his scientific life, he seems to jump from one topic or field to another. This life has been guided by his interests (aquaculture, aquarium technology, husbandry and disease of captive marine mammals and fishes, marine environmental physiology, and coral reef ecology) and marine and freshwater field experiences in his travels to Brazil (Rondônia, Roraima, Amazonas); Canadian lower arctic (Hudson's Bay); Alaska (Bering Sea); Canadian Maritime Provinces; Ecuador; California; Pacific Northwest (Oregon, Washington, British Columbia); México (both coasts); Florida Keys and northern Gulf of Mexico; New England; Central America (Atlantic coast); British, French, and Dutch West Indies; US and British Virgin Islands; Philippines (South China Sea, Sulu Sea); and wow! South Pacific (Cook Islands, French Polynesia, Solomon Islands). He even holds a US Merchant Marine officer's license.

He started publishing in the scientific literature by providing technical information necessary to maintain fledgling public aquaria, including that involving husbandry and health of marine mammals. Not only did he conduct research, but he curated the Aquarium of Niagara Falls, Niagara Falls, New York, and New York Aquarium, Wildlife Conservation Society, Brooklyn, New York; served as Executive Director of the Mystic Aquarium, Mystic, Connecticut; and Vice President of Aquarium Systems, Inc., Mentor, Ohio.

He got the itch to study biodiversity and symbiosis of tropical organisms in the wild, so he became Director and Principal Investigator of the Turks and Caicos Islands Coral Reef Ecology Program funded through the Oakleigh L. Thorne Foundation in New York City. During his trips, he ran the Foundation to survey the area, working hard every day and keeping his employees in "line." He is well known for being hardnosed about productivity and maintaining safety of the scuba divers. There was considerable deep diving and underwater photographing, and Steve became a world authority on commensal shrimp before moving on to his next adventure. Actually, at the same time he became Director of Research, Sea Research Foundation, Noank, Connecticut, and Research Scientist, Marine Sciences & Technology Center, The University of Connecticut at Avery Point, Groton, Connecticut. Since

2001 he has been Adjunct Scientist, Mote Marine Laboratory, Sarasota, Florida. While in Florida, he decided to create a home garden but encountered some difficulties. So what did he do? He shared his acquired knowledge in a book (*Coastal Florida Gardening: A Botanical Perspective*).

Because of his widespread knowledge about constructing public aquaria and maintaining living displays, he has used his business acumen in consulting. He provided information for well-known public aquariums in ten states as well as for ventures in four countries abroad. His efforts have also had a significant positive impact on entertainment displays. For a few months, Steve visited Mississippi's Gulf coast to design a system for Donald Trump's envisioned dolphinarium. Although plans fell through, I was fortunate enough to share lunches, laughs, and ideas during those trips.

Much of Steve's success results from considerable effort. He does not waste time; he is always productive writing, investigating, inventing, or appreciating. Born in 1942, he grew up in a coal mining camp in southern West Virginia, learning life from close associations with people and activities there and aboard boats, in jungles, on beaches, in aquaculture facilities, in the research laboratories, and behind his typewriter or computer.

I first met Steve early in his career when he curated aquariums. Later, when I presented a scientific talk in Groton, I finally got the opportunity to visit him at his home. He asked where I would like to eat. In a joking fashion I said, "Mystic Pizza" because I had enjoyed the 1988 movie starring Annabeth Gish. He said, "Grab your coat," and, to my astonishment, we walked around the corner to where there existed an actual Mystic Pizza; Steve personally knew all the employees in that quaint little restaurant with its entrance to the kitchen on the opposite side as it occurred in the movie.

Steve is certainly never afraid to expose his weaknesses. He does this in *My Watery Self,* as he did in *The Smoking Horse.* More important, he shows his strong love of life, including music, literature, science, and history. He always digs to the depths of any of those foundations, which necessitates a firm knowledge of the "participants" of each field on a first name basis acquired in the field, workplace, bar, or neighborhood.

Most scientists do not write memoirs, especially ones that might make the reader wonder, with all the associated "wild" experiences with alcohol and chemicals, how the biographer ever became a bonafide professional scientist. This book follows *The Smoking Horse,* with a spectrum of thrills. Young potential scientists today must get involved with marine science through a good education rather than random experiences. I know; I entered the field slowly, being spurred into action by reading *Cannery Row*, experiencing adventures in a small fishing community similar to those of Steve, seeing absurd but captivating behaviors of renowned scientists at meetings, observing many unexpected animals and behaviors, and enjoying my honeymoon searching marked snails with my wife on the unpopulated-at-the-time beach of North Key Largo, Steve's country.

In the introduction to his book, *Coastal Florida Gardening: A Botanical Perspective*, Steve notes, "We buy books for two reasons: to entertain us and to increase our knowledge of the world. I found out a long time ago that if I learned one useful thing from a book it had been worth the price." In the case of *My Watery Self*, with its many wonderful short stories, the entire book fulfills both reasons, providing several very useful things and plenty of laughs.

For instance, did you know that silvery-colored fishes contain crystals of guanine that reflect and refract light? Well, if that refraction shows that the intensity of horizontal light reflected back from the fish is the same as the background light, the fish would be invisible. With that knowledge Steve learned to stalk and spear large striped bass.

In Key Largo, Steve frequented Sarge's on Friday evening for his uncrowded establishment with all-you-can-eat fried grouper and French fries for $1.25 and draft beer for half price. When the tarpon started jumping and smacking water with their sides, Steve described it as "From sea level, you couldn't get any closer to heaven." You will find out how Sarge got rid of patrons after receiving an exceptional newspaper review that attracted way too many unwanted customers.

How would you transfer a heavy, stranded pygmy sperm whale and her calf from the beach to an exhibit at the New York Aquarium at Coney Island? Stephen Spotte knows. Moreover, he knows how to use cunning psychological methods to keep from getting mugged on his nightly treks to the Aquarium to feed the calf. Hold on to appreciate the development and adventures of a real marine biologist.

—*Robin M. Overstreet, PhD*
*Professor Emeritus, Department of Coastal Sciences*
*University of Southern Mississippi*
*Ocean Springs, MS*

## Publications by Stephen Spotte

Scientific books written by Stephen Spotte for academic readers include *Tarpon Biology [In progress]*; *Free-ranging Cats: Biology, Ecology, Management.* Wiley-Blackwell (2014); *Societies of Wolves and Free-ranging Dogs.* Cambridge University Press (2012); *Coastal Florida Gardening: A Botanical Perspective.* CreateSpace.com (2009); *Bluegills: Biology and Behavior.* American Fisheries Society (2007); *Zoos in Postmodernism: Signs and Simulation.* Fairleigh Dickinson University Press, (2006, cultural theory); *Candiru: Life and Legend of the Bloodsucking Catfishes.* Creative Arts Books (2002); *Captive Seawater Fishes: Science and Technology.* John Wiley & Sons (1992); *Sterilization of Marine Mammal Pool Waters: Theoretical and Health Considerations.* Technical Bulletin Number 1797, USDA (1991); *Artificial Seawaters: Formulas and Methods.* Jones & Bartlett (Bidwell and Spotte, 1985); *Seawater Aquariums: The Captive Environment.* John Wiley & Sons (1979); and *Fish and Invertebrate Culture: Water Management in Closed Systems.* John Wiley & Sons (1970, 1979, Russian edition 1983).

He also wrote scientific books for the general public, including *Marine Aquarium Keeping: The Science, Animals, and Art.* John Wiley & Sons (1973, 1993, September 1973 Main Selection, Natural Sciences Book Club, a division of Book-of-the-Month Club; Chinese edition 1977) and *Secrets of the Deep.* Charles Scribner's Sons (1976, December 1976 Alternate Selection, Natural Science Book Club, a division of Book-of-the-Month Club).

In addition, he has published a variety of fiction and creative nonfiction books, including *Cantor's Theorem and Other Stories* (2013); *Brother's Ghost: A Novella.* Northwestern University Press (2011); *The Smoking Horse: A Memoir in Pieces.* SUNY Press (2010, creative nonfiction); *Home is the Sailor, Under the Sea: Mermaid Stories.* Creative Arts Book Company (2000); *An Optimist in Hell: Stories.* Creative Arts Book Company (1998).

# *Redhorse Blues*

On an afternoon in early autumn just after school started, I was killing time standing on the bank of Huff Creek a couple of hundred feet from our house. I must have been twelve or thirteen. The day was warm. I'd just climbed down from the school bus and walked home, depressed over the thought of another year of classes. Back then in 1955, I was living in a company house with my parents and baby sister in Mallory, a coal camp in southern West Virginia not far from Kentucky.

Huff Creek was always black with the coal dust that emptied into it upstream from a tipple where coal dug from the mines was crushed and washed before being loaded onto trains. These went wheezing and wobbling slowly past my bedroom window at all hours, their whistles blowing every few seconds to warn trackwalkers and drunks to step aside.

The creek was shallow and sluggish from lack of late-summer rain, and instead of resembling liquid tar, on this day the water was a translucent, sickening gray. Only the submerged objects—mostly rocks, discarded tires, and parts of wrecked cars—were black and slimed over. Tipple effluent was polluted and acidic, and seeing a fish, crayfish, or any living creature in the receiving stream was a rare event. But on that day, in the middle of the creek not eight feet from the bank, a huge redhorse finned slowly in place, facing the current. It must have been a foot long and weighed at least a pound. A redhorse is a species of bottom-feeding minnow common to Appalachian streams and rivers. Nobody eats them much, and they aren't famous for being caught on hooks because they grub around in the gravel, ingesting tiny aquatic insects and crustaceans.

I ran home and got my cane pole, baited the hook with a small earthworm, and gave it a try anyway. With fishing you never know. The worm drifted right past the fish's nose. For a couple of hours I tried to catch that redhorse, but nothing worked. Finally Mama opened the back door and called me to supper. The next day another kid my age who lived in the camp came up and asked what I was doing. His name might have been Earl. I pointed to the fish, barely visible against the black gunk. He looked at it and walked away.

Catching that fish became an obsession to which I devoted all my spare time. I tried everything as bait, including table scraps and tiny insects I caught in the field near the train tracks and underneath rocks. Grasshoppers and crickets were common in late summer, and I tried those too. I switched hooks systematically, going down one size each day until I was left with only the smallest bream hooks in my arsenal, but the effort was useless.

It was odd how the fish never changed location. It lay there finning itself into the current, shifting a few inches now and then, but never really going anywhere, and my intrusions were nothing but a minor annoyance. I would go down to the creek early in the morning before school, later when school was out, and again after supper before dark. This continued for three weeks or so.

Then on a Saturday morning, on my way to the creek, I saw this same kid, Earl, hauling out a huge fish, certainly the biggest to come out of Huff Creek in recent memory. My redhorse!

"I snared him," Earl said. "I throwed out a treble hook, drug the line acrost him real slow, and then jerked it. Didn't need no bait." The smirk he showed was unbearable.

"That's my fish," I said, and shoved him hard. I was taller, but he was tough and wiry and shoved me back.

I punched him in the nose, gratified to see blood. He launched a roundhouse that caught me on the ear, making it sting mightily. I tossed a straight right at the instant he ducked his head. Instead of connecting with a soft nose or lip, I missed his face completely and hit solid bone, feeling pain radiate from my hand all the way to the shoulder.

I ignored the pain and punched him a good one in the gut. By then we were scuffed up and sweating hard there on the creek bank, flattening out the goldenrod and burdock around us in a ragged circle. We had been chewing tobacco and were leaking and slobbering brown juice over each other like a couple of mating grasshoppers, turning whatever blood there was on our clothes to the color of shit. Add to that a substantial breading of dirt and sand tinted by weed stains.

After we'd grappled and thrashed on the ground a respectable time, Earl said he wanted to quit and go home, a suggestion I went along with. We had been fighting on top of the fish, which was now mangled beyond recognition, and the treble hooks had become caught on my pants. We had to rip them out. He took the remains of the fish and left.

I'D LEARNED ABOUT REDHORSES FIVE years earlier when my family had lived in another part of the state and

Daddy worked a different mine. We lived in an isolated house at the time, practically across the street from the mine entrance, and Daddy could walk to work carrying his lunch bucket. I had no one to play with, but up a dirt road not quite a half-mile away was a farm where Mr. and Mrs. Howard lived with their ten kids. The two youngest were boys. Millard was my age, about seven or eight, and Dewey was two years older. We became a threesome, and I often got off the school bus and walked home with them to play around the barns and other outbuildings. The Howards grew crops and raised domestic animals and were mostly self-sufficient.

There were several older daughters who looked after us occasionally until, one by one, they each acquired kids of their own to chase after.

Mr. H had never finished grade school, but he was widely read and fancied himself an expert on many things, including Shakespeare, the dictionary, and West Virginia's natural history. He could gut and skin a deer quick as lightning, and have slices of venison jerky curing over smoke within the hour. For smokers he had two junk refrigerators with their bottoms ripped out, set off the ground on cinder blocks. He used the metal shelves inside to lay the meat on, and he built smoldering hickory fires underneath. The smoke rose inside the refrigerators and emerged through drill holes in the tops.

Mr. H recognized all the useful plants that grew wild in the surrounding hills and hollows, and in summer he sent Dewey, Millard, and me into the fields and woods to dig roots of chicory for "hillbilly coffee"; goldenseal and sassafras for various remedies, teas, and tonics; and ginseng, the most valuable herb of all. Ginseng was worth a lot, and Mr. H sold his in town and used the cash to buy sugar and coffee and other goods he couldn't grow on the farm. On days when we seemed bored and out of sorts, Mr. H would suggest we go "sangin'" in the woods. He said he could always use more "root," by which he meant ginseng, to sell in town, and he advised us to look for it growing beneath butternut trees. By then we could recognize the edible and medicinal plants ourselves. We were barefoot and barely taller than a standing shovel, but sangin' never seemed like work to us. The woods were where we wanted to be anyway.

In autumn we competed with the squirrels to gather hickory nuts, walnuts, and butternuts, and in squirrel season we shot squirrels, which Mrs. H stuffed with stale bread and spices and the nuts we'd found, and baked slathered with fresh butter made from goat milk. For side dishes there were canned fruits and vegetables put up by Mrs. H and her daughters as soon as produce on the farm became available for canning, or wild fruits like pawpaws, raspberries and blackberries, wild cherries, and crab apples, which could be picked in the woods and fields. Their cellar, adjacent to the coal bin, seemed to me a dim crypt of endless shelves stocked with jars of preserves and bins of tubers.

On snowy days after school we shelled nuts for Mrs. H to put into cookies, and we drank sassafras tea to "purify the blood" while awaiting homemade bread to emerge from the oven. A home remedy was always available for what ailed us or to take as a preventative. There were cow-manure poultices for sprains and bruises and the liquid from boiled poke-weed leaves as a tonic to restore the blood in spring. In the fall, just before school started, Mrs. H and Mama wormed us by administering us two table-spoons of turpentine each.

In winter while the older boys were outside doing chores, Mr. H read Shakespeare to us, and if Mama was there the two of them would argue about words. Mama had some education and was of the opinion that just because a word is in the dictionary didn't mean it was a good word, that the dictionary listed all the words in English, including some that weren't meant to be spoken. Swear words, for example. Mr. H disagreed. In particular, he said it was okay to use "ain't" exactly because it's in the dictionary, and why would the dictionary include words nobody could use? As I remember, they never reached an agreement, and I was allowed to use "ain't" at Dewey and Millard's house but not mine, and the same held true for them.

In winter the creeks froze, denying me access to water and inducing an odd feeling of derealization when normal sensations received from the waking world arrived glazed over and incomplete. At such times I envied the squirrels and groundhogs hibernating until spring. Dewey and Millard seemed not to notice, and to adults I probably came across as hyperactive or maybe just weird.

My relief until warm weather came around was the Howards' springhouse. This was a separate building—a shed, actually—a few steps from their main house, used for dipping up drinking water and as a ready source of refrigeration. Frigid water from an underground spring seeped up through the earth, forming a shallow pool inside the springhouse from which the overflow tumbled across a low spillway into a nearby creek. Even in midsummer the water felt icy, and Mrs. H kept her cow and goat milk and the butter she churned in crocks submerged in it.

The pool, dark except for what little daylight leaked through cracks in the walls and roof, also served as a holding area for live fish caught with our cane poles and snapping turtles the older boys brought home from their trotlines. The fish were mostly bluegills from the pasture pond, and for a family the size of the Howards a lot were needed to make a meal. When enough had been accumulated, the three of us were dispatched to the springhouse to net out the fish and clean them. Mr. H or one of the older boys caught and butchered the turtles. Then Mrs. H and her daughters rolled the fish and skinless turtle legs in raw egg and flour and fried everything in a big cast iron skillet using bacon grease saved from their own slaughtered hogs.

During one of those events I learned about the redhorse. Mr. H said it belonged to the sucker family, and you could tell a redhorse from other suckers by its red-tinted tail. Suckers were cousins to the carp, he said, bottom-feeders and not especially tasty, although he'd eaten them in a pinch and they weren't too bad with a side of boiled fresh dandelion greens topped with hot bacon grease and a little dandelion vinegar. Because they were usually small you had to fry them whole, and it took a mess of suckers to make a decent meal.

A few days before this conversation, Dewey, Millard, and I had been building a dam in the creek and trapped a redhorse. We put it in a bucket and went to ask Mr. H what kind of fish it was, but he was out somewhere in the fields, so we released it in the springhouse and forgot about it until it was time to catch and clean the rest of the fish. Then up it came in the net. Our specimen was small, the length of a finger.

According to Mr. H the sucker stood in God's chain of life halfway between the carp and the catfish, having fewer whiskers than the catfish. Mr. H taught us that a hog's bristles were halfway, too, after their own fashion, being neither fur nor hair, and as proof just try making a shaving brush out of either. Mr. H had a shaving brush he'd made himself using bristles from one of his scalded hogs and set with glue in a carved cherry wood handle. The years and oils from his hand had polished it to a dull sunset glow.

Nearly every day I'm reminded of that scuffle with Earl when the knuckle just above my index finger starts to pain me and I need to soak it in hot water. It all happened under an irresolute blue sky with no witnesses except ourselves. I reach for a towel and hope that Earl has a permanent lump on his forehead.

# *Exercises on a Tightrope*

THE CARNIVAL CAME THAT SUMMER and set up in a vacant field, tent pegs hammered into dry clay among the discarded tires and other trash. It was late August, a time when the early sun felt suddenly cooler, radiating a feel of autumn. Morning mist hung in the air above the creek, black with coal dust, imparting a false hope of transparency to the water underneath. Sassafras and sumac had already turned scarlet on the mountains, their twitching leaves oozing like a wind-blown river into the hollows.

I thumbed into town early that Saturday. Alvin and Grady and some of the others would be there eventually. We were interested in seeing if the carnival had any morphodites on display and would later sneak into the strip show. Those were our main objectives, aside from looking at the girls and drinking some beer. There was no gate where you paid a general admission, so I walked around the place watching the workers getting ready to open. A lion roared from somewhere, but otherwise there were just human voices. They had one big tent set up in the middle with lesser tents and other attractions spaced around it like satellites. I went inside and looked at the ring where the barker would stand surrounded by the chairs in which the spectators would sit. Overhead was a tightrope with ladders on each end topped off by platforms. I had two dollars in loose cash and planned to stay all day and well into the evening.

Just as I was coming out of the big tent an old man stopped me by putting his hand gently on my chest.

"Where you going, sonny?" he asked. He was stooped and wrinkled and weighed maybe a hundred pounds. I could have walked right through his arm if I'd wanted, but I didn't out of politeness and the thought that maybe I was trespassing. A faint stink came off him, lingering and hesitant, like a lurking dampness of swamp. Tucked under it was that smell of liquor so long in the body it becomes part of the sweat. I glanced down at the hand set to hold me back. It was a chicken's foot—long thin fingers yellowed from nicotine and topped by scraggly claws.

"I'm just looking around, seeing what I can see," I answered.

"And what do you see?"

"I see an empty tent with some chairs and a tight-rope. I guess it'll be full of people later on."

"Well, that ain't the all of it, just what you think you see." He had a hill accent and had probably grown up around here in Logan County or somewhere over the state line in Kentucky. He took his hand away. "That's because wherever this tent goes there's stories that goes with it. Everywhere—it don't matter even if it went to China, the ground it's on ain't what counts, nor the tent, just the stories. And if this tent was to burn down and another put up, it'd be the same. Now you look like a curious boy. Let's go inside and I'll tell you one of them stories. Interested?"

"Sure," I said. I had nothing else to do. We went inside the big tent and sat in two chairs at ringside. He bummed a cigarette and leaned back. It was like dusk in there without the lights on, our backs to the glare from the one opening. The metal folding chairs had been kicked around until the padding was gone from the seats, leaving only dried glue. In the oblique light you could see stretch marks in the tent fabric and some dark spots where someone had patched it; in other places it was worn thin and a little sunlight glowered through.

He sat a while and smoked, then told me he'd run away from home at about twelve and had worked for circuses and carnivals ever since. In his prime, that had been roustabout work, but he was too old now and taken to washing dishes in the pie wagon for room and board. Sometimes the boss threw a little cigarette money his way, but he wasn't complaining. He had food, a bed, and a roof to sleep under, and the life had mostly been good. I had started looking around, and he probably sensed the waning interest. He asked my age and I told him fourteen, but I lied.

"Can you see that tightrope?" He pointed up.

"I see it alright," I said. "I can see there's nobody on it."

From inside his coveralls the old man took out a pint bottle. It was clear glass without a label, and the liquor inside it was clear too. He unscrewed the cap and took a swallow. He probably had sources and kept refilling the same bottle until the label had finally rubbed off in his pocket. No telling what had been kept in it over the years. "Want a nip of moonshine?" he asked. I took a swallow that watered my eyes like wringing out a wet rag, but he pretended not to notice. I coughed and held out the bottle, which was oddly smooth, oily almost, from years of service. His scrawny chicken hand reached over and clutched it.

"There's nobody on that wire now, but one time there was—a real lady."

"Won't a wirewalker be up on it today?" I asked.

"Oh sure," he replied, "one of them kids that don't know the history of the perfession and don't care shit excepting to gain a paycheck. Then they run off and next you hear the girls is knocked up and tending register at the five and dime. Since her I ain't even bothered to learn their names. It ain't nothing to be a wirewalker these days, but that wasn't always true." I shook two cigarettes up from my pack and we each took one.

"It was a long, long time ago, sonny." He turned and looked at me. I could see the separation that age had made in his rheumy eyes. His back or leg must have ached because he kept shifting in the chair. He produced the pint and we each enjoyed a jolt. "Matter of fact," he said, "it was back about nineteen-hundred and aught-two or maybe three, I can't hardly remember now. So far back it don't mean anything to someone your age.

"Anyhow, I'd been with the same circus for maybe ten years and moving around pretty good, mostly all over the South. It was nice work, roustabouting, and I was young and strong, like nothing could ever hurt me. Every setup and teardown was pure hustle, driving them tent pegs or yanking them out, pulling on canvas, and the boys hollering insults at one another, all in good fun, a'course, although we did have our differences now and again, and I got me some lumps and scars to prove it.

"Sonny, there wasn't nothing like circus life. New girls in every town, pretty ones too, and sometimes they cried when we was pulling up stakes and wanted to come along, but it would never have worked out. The circus is its own family, and you got to like that life on the move. Most women don't, and even when they cried we knowed they was better off when we left them behind.

"It was in Memphis where this group of wirewalkers joined up. They was from a old German circus family, second generation in America, and perfessional all the way. The main walkers was the four youngsters, all of them in their twenties, three young men and a girl. At the audition there was nobody but circus folk, and we're a skeptical lot, but after watching their act we was dumbfounded. Them boys throwed their sister all to hell and back, I mean up in the air and all, and just when you figured she's a goner one of the brothers reaches out at the last second and grabs her hand and swings her back up where she lands on the wire standing straight. They made it look dangerous but it was all part of the act, you see. They knowed every second where she would be flying by. And they could walk that wire too, one atop the other 'til they was all four stacked up like playing cards. And the bottom one riding a bicycle to boot. The rest of us had never seen nothing like it.

"The girl was pretty, but not what you'd call beautiful. She was real limber and could backwalk down the wire, stand on her hands, and so forth. They didn't ask much of us except that one roustabout be assigned to wire maintenance. They give that job to me for some reason. After setup I was to climb up one of the ladders and set the tightness of the wire using a pry bar pushed through a turnbuckle. Know what that is?" I shook my head. He explained it, and how the wire could be made tight or loose depending on whether you made the turnbuckle go clockwise or counterclockwise.

"One of the brothers always come around and checked my work. He'd stand on the platform and put one foot on the wire and push real hard, then he'd walk out a ways and start pumping it to beat hell, jumping up and down 'til it wobbled like a guitar string that was strung real tight. It was the slack in the wire that caused it to wobble and made you lose balance. After a few weeks I got the hang and done it perfect. Just the right amount of tightness. It was like a art, and them folks appreciated it, let me tell you. They had blonde hair and blue eyes, same as all Germans, I reckon.

"They'd been with us maybe two months. We was setting up in Birmingham. After I tightened the wire and had it strung just right the girl come up on the platform and touched my shoulder. For two months we hadn't said a word to one another, just a glance here and there.

She was dressed for the show, even though it wasn't for another three hours or so. She looked beautiful with her makeup, and she smelled like a whole valley of flowers. I couldn't stop looking at her. Well, she kept her hand on my shoulder and told me how she appreciated what I'd been doing for her and her kin, that I made their job less dangerous. She said I made her feel safe, that she was glad it was me tending to the wire and not someone else, another roustabout. She asked if I'd stick around while she tried some new exercises.

"I said sure, I'd be happy to. I was already crazy in love. You ever been in love, sonny?" I shook my head. "Well, he continued, it's fun for a time and then it ain't. I ast if she didn't need the net underneath because it was all new, her exercises, but she said no, that without that net she had to pay closer attention and it made her alert. So I climbed down from the platform and stood there in the sawdust looking up at her and getting a crick in my neck. I figured later I'd go see the circus doc, who'd tell me to tie a piece of red flannel cloth around it. My mama had always said that a better cure for a crick is to go rub your neck on a fence where a hog had just rubbed, but our circus didn't have no hogs.

"The wire itself was near invisible against the darkness, and she looked like a butterfly flitting around on air. It was all a dream to me except better, being I was awake. And when she finished she stood on the platform and leaned over and blowed me a kiss. Shit, I could of walked that wire myself right then, I felt so light."

He produced the bottle, and we each took a healthy swallow and lit up. I was getting a little drunk and it wasn't even nine o'clock in the morning.

It felt good, and I knew my friends would be jealous when they saw me staggering a little. The old man pushed back his hat, an old felt job looking like it came off a plow mule. Outside, men were yelling about this or that, circus lingo I couldn't understand. There were also some foreigners talking in something that wasn't English.

"That routine of theirs went on for a couple of months," the old man said. His voice startled me, although he'd only been silent a minute or two. "Before exercising she always came and found me, and I went along to the wire following like a puppy dog. The boys took to teasing me, and for once I didn't get mad. I kind of liked it, in fact. 'There goes your girlfriend,' one would say. That talk always made my face red. If we was pitching hay, for example, they'd see me turn red as a hanky and then they'd laugh and punch me on the shoulder, but in a friendly way. And the girl, she started looking at me different. Her eyes was softer in a way I can't explain, and she always smiled whenever I come around, like she was waiting for me and nobody else.

"And then it was Chattanooga, I recall clear as Christmas, we was standing on the platform all by ourself, and she raised up on her tippy toes and kissed me, and you better believe I kissed her back. I ain't never had a kiss like that before or since."

He looked over at me. "You ever been kissed, sonny?" I nodded, but we thought of it as just swapping spit, something girls insisted on before letting you grab a little sweater tit or rub a bare knee. "Here," he said, "have a swallower. You got another of them smokes on you?"

I didn't own a watch, but the light behind seemed brighter. He settled back. "We went on like that," he said, "grabbing at one another and kissing every opportunity—on the platform, in a dark corner of the tent, out behind the pie wagon—anywhere nobody's around to see. People knowed, a'course. You can't keep a secret from circus folk, not with all them people living close together like that. Nobody seemed to mind. Why, when I laid in bed just thinking about her near give me what you youngsters call a organism.

"I figured she was better than me, being from a long line of trained performers, sort of like royalty. Me? I was just a roustabout, a nobody. I wouldn't of knowed my own parents if I bumped directly into them. Me and her had long since spoke our love for one another. Whenever I seen her I got this jump in my chest, like something had popped out and left a hole. I thought maybe I was sick, but the doc said I had a heart strong as a tiger's and not to worry. We always had a doc along, usually one leaving a problem behind.

"She looked at me like I was special. No one ever done that before or since, as if it was just the two of us. When she held my hand hers was little but real strong, and she had near as many calluses as me, but hers come from gripping that wire and spinning around on it and such. And each day we wasn't on the move she exercised while I watched from below. She was trying out new tricks for their act, and the exercises got more and more dangerous. Maybe she thought I was her net, ready to catch her if she fell, and a'course I'd of done it or died trying. There she'd be turning cartwheels and spinning around, so graceful, each movement the most beautiful thing you could imagine. She was perfect, sonny. Perfect as perfection gets.

"We took to eating all our meals together in the pie wagon, sitting side by side, and she liked to grab my hand under the table and squeeze it hard. She had little hands and looked nice and soft, all them curves, but she was hard all over and strong as hell. And she hardly ate anything. Said she had to keep her figure, that it was curtains if she ever got flabby. 'You ever seen a fat person walk the wire?' she'd ask. After supper we'd stroll around a little in good weather, looking at the stars and such and kissing.

"We took the circus to Maine that summer, to a place by the seashore. I'd never seed the ocean before. Her and me took to going down to sit by it in our spare time, and the noise the waves made was so loud we could hardly hear one another. The rocks, they was wet and slippery as creek rocks, but bigger, some bigger than trailer trucks, and green weeds was stuck on them that waved back and forth when the water moved. All kinds of shells grew on the rocks, and at night you'd hear what the locals called a foghorn way out somewhere warning ships not to come close for they'd sink sure as hell. And the fog was so thick—just a step below rain.

"One night we was walking in the dunes back of the beach, and I stopped and picked some daisies and handed them to her. I'd never picked a flower in my life, never even noticed them before. They was just splotches of color here and there. She held them flowers like they might of been diamonds or rubies. She told me that the flowers wouldn't live long even in water, but she now had this memory of them and things once in memory never die. And she said something else. She said that when two people in love have the same memory, that's best of all because they can enjoy it forever. She teased me and said, 'Now you better not forget this night and these flowers,' and I promised I wouldn't. Then she done something I thought peculiar. She showed me two flowers with a petal missing. Flawed, I think she called them, but still beautiful together, just like us.

"That fall we'd come onto this field outside of Valdosta and finished setting up when some old boys I knowed from years past showed up and started hollering at me to go get a drink. I went and told my girl. She give me a big kiss and said to behave and have a good time, so off I went. Well, we done a major crawl through all the bars and they dumped me off near daylight drunk as a pig. I laid down on my bunk and slept like a dead toad.

"Next I knowed some roustabouts was shaking me awake, saying there'd been a accident. I run over to the big tent and pushed through the gawkers and seen my girl laying on the ground. I grabbed her hand. She was all broke up and bleeding. I leaned down and she said in a whisper, 'I waited for you. . . .'

"I looked up at the wire and must of went deaf. Not the sirens nor the hollering jarred me out of it, and the place seemed still and cold as if I was underwater and starving for air. I looked at my girl and that special thing was gone from her eyes, that something shiny like a pond or a camera's eye where your picture's reflected back. There's no sense blaming today on yesterday because it won't make tomorrow any easier. But it's hard, sonny, it's hard. . . ."

I felt dizzy and closed in, but the old man's adventures had also imparted a weightless feeling, as if I could jump straight up and touch the top of the tent. At the same time the image of the girl wouldn't go away. I saw her dying underneath that tightrope on cheap ground raked over by roustabouts and layered in sawdust. The old man was crying without any noise of it, just the sight of his shoulders humping up and down. They looked weak and ineffectual like wings of a bug against a screen door.

The bottle lay on the chair between us. I unscrewed it and took a big swallow, feeling as if something warm with recent life had just blown through my soul. It's strange how a story can become a part of you. Most are forgotten, but some, like this one, you wear like a second skin the rest of your life. Maybe the only way it ever balanced out was to tell others what you heard and add something of yourself, and if you lived long enough everything else might fall away.

I couldn't blot the girl and the sea out of my mind, and I knew I had to get there someday, to feel the surge and hear the foghorn, drink in the mist, maybe pick a daisy under furtive moonlight and hand it to a girl of my own. I touched the old man's shoulder. "I've got to go," I said. It wasn't true, but I knew if I didn't leave right then I might never go back to that sad creek black with coal dust.

# *Memories of Flight*

THEIR NAMES WERE GEORGE AND Sherryn. They were married to each other and had a little son of maybe three or four. I don't remember his name. I was eighteen or nineteen, and who can recall that sort of thing from that time in your life? He was a typical rug rat except for a congenital malady of an intestinal nature. Everybody was always worrying over whether he'd taken a successful shit and, if he had, bending down close to examine the result. I think George and Sherryn were in their early thirties, although they could have been younger.

We were all at the Jersey shore working dead-end jobs. It was the summer of '60 or '61. George was painting houses, and Sherryn was trying to be a wife and mother. They had a little rental place on Atlantic Avenue. I was lifeguarding south of Beach Haven and living with several other derelicts in the attic of a rooming house. Two of them were Cap and Uncle Dirty. Cap waited tables at a restaurant named Gus and Whitey's; Uncle Dirty had discovered a way of collecting unemployment despite not having held a job in recent memory. He spent most days in the attic practicing his saxophone and nights practicing getting drunk.

George was a skinny guy, bearded and soft-spoken, with the stoned empty stare of a prophet. He'd once seen the face of Jesus in a pizza, dripping tears of mozzarella from pepperoni eyes. He lived mostly in his painting clothes, which acquired spatters of new color with every house he painted. By Labor Day he looked like a traveling replica of Willem de Kooning's Door to the River, except shaggy at the top and with a pair of tanned feet sticking out the bottom.

We drank a lot of alcoholic beverages and took drugs, and all of us except George spent time at the beach hustling coeds. As to the last activity, girl-watching was part of a lifeguard's routine. I was working at the beach six days a week between nine and five-thirty. In the off-hours and my single free day I spearfished and surfed.

Large striped bass often schooled at the end of the jetty at the beach I guarded, and spearing them was a challenge. They were wary, strong, and quick to disappear. A few guys I knew had managed to spear the occasional laggard with a spear gun, but I had only a fiberglass pole spear powered by a loop of surgical tubing tied to one end. You "cocked" the pole by putting the loop across the meaty part of your hand between the thumb and base of the forefinger, then sliding your hand up the pole and gripping it tightly. To "fire" the spear you aimed down your extended arm and released your hand, letting the rubber tubing propel the pole forward. The pole was four feet long, which meant that you needed to be within three feet or so of the fish. Stalking a wary striper underwater while holding your breath and wearing snorkeling gear and flippers isn't easy.

My first summer at the beach I struck out. Underwater visibility varied with weather and tides, but even in clear water during late afternoon, when I ordinarily spearfished after the beaches closed, a large striper could vanish from view simply by moving a few inches away. I wondered how this was possible. Sometimes when I could bum a ride I hunted around the rocks at Barnegat Light at the north end of Long Beach Island. There were always tautogs weighing a pound or two lurking in the crevices and big stripers cruising the shoreline. On days when the water was especially clear and the tide was coming in from the Atlantic, you saw the silhouettes of sharks drifting with the current like ghostly torpedoes into Barnegat Bay.

Back at school I checked out library books on ichthyology and undersea optics. The first explained that skins of silvery fishes like stripers contain crystals of guanine that reflect and refract light. The second showed that if the intensity of horizontal light reflected back from the fish was the same as the light in the background (in oceanography called the background spacelight), the fish would become invisible, vanishing into its own image. I now knew how these factors worked in concert, and during the next summer I became proficient at stalking and spearing stripers, which the landlady let us attic denizens bake in her oven.

One day I dragged back a twenty-pounder. The other boarders chipped in with salads, baking potatoes, bread, beer, and wine, and everyone joined the feast, including our landlady and her family.

I also dabbled in chemistry using the kitchen as a laboratory. I taught myself to concoct homemade LSD, cheered on by my roommates, who seemed unduly impressed that I was attending college, and especially that among the subjects I studied were chemistry and biology.

Uncle Dirty had a motor scooter. We drove it over to the mainland on one of my days off and went shopping. The list included a measuring cup with a metric scale on one side, a sack of morning glory seeds, petroleum ether, drugstore alcohol, and a box of empty gelatin capsules. In those days, none of these items was illegal, but later it became nearly impossible to buy morning glory seeds. A scale to weigh stuff would have been helpful, but we couldn't find one small enough. I used the landlady's kitchen scale instead, extrapolating weight measures as best I could. Petroleum ether was the most expensive purchase. I forget what it cost, but it seemed a lot. For glassware I had only to open the kitchen cupboard.

Back at the rooming house I fumbled initially with different measures using notes scribbled from texts in the chemistry library at school. Each snippet described just a step or two of the sequence and focused mainly on reactions and reaction rates, not the manufacturing. A stoner chemistry student showed up on my beach one day. We got to talking. He was in the middle of a prolonged stay in graduate school, hoping to avoid the draft. He was making drugs of various sorts for side money, including LSD, and helped complete some of the blank spaces in my notes.

Basically you ground about five ounces (by weight) of seeds to powder, which you soaked in petroleum ether and afterward squeezed through a piece of nylon stocking. After evaporating the remaining liquid you soaked the residue in alcohol and let that evaporate, then repeated this step. Here and there was some pouring of liquids back and forth. It was useful not to be too stoned or drunk because sometimes the residue got thrown away and sometimes the liquid. It was important to remember which.

Each evaporation took a couple of days, the entire sequence a week or so. I used our attic roof underneath a protected eave as the evaporator. My roomies visited the roof often—which could be done by stepping out a window—gazing tenderly at the row of cereal bowls with their mysterious contents. It was like keeping a pregnant woman up there, everyone waiting nervously for the birth.

Parturition produced some yellow gummy-looking crap that I scraped into a few capsules. You popped one and shortly after the gelatin dissolved and just before lift-off came a sudden and uncontrollable retching. Because the method and measurements were inexact, no one knew what sort of trip to expect. Each flight soared into uncharted worlds. After landing, I was always slightly awed that none of us had died or done something truly stupid, like try to slow-dance with a moving bus.

One trip did disrupt the balance of our restricted world. One evening, our group swallowed caps of my homemade concoction in George and Sherryn's living room. Sherryn didn't drop LSD, feeling she needed to be coherent because of her son's medical condition, although she never turned down a toke. I recall her walking back and forth in shorts, barefoot, carrying a laundry basket. Sherryn had a glass eye from a childhood disease. Uncle Dirty had evidently been watching too, and the sight of her glass eye, her legs, and the laundry basket set him to bawling. "It's so beautiful," he said, and he kept repeating it. "What?" someone asked through the mind-haze. "Oh, sweet Jesus, you have to ask? You really have to ask? My god, he has to ask." He kept going on. Why do I remember? Because I'd delayed dropping my own cap. I was worrying that maybe I'd fucked up this batch of acid and thought I should wait and see whether anyone suffered a grand mal seizure or permanent retardation and I'd need to roust the EMTs. The lifeguards, cops, fire fighters, and emergency medical personnel worked for the Township of Long Beach Island. Lots of us knew each other.

Everyone survived including me, needless to say. The image of Sherryn and her glass eye doing laundry became, to Uncle Dirty, the apotheosis of womanhood, and he was instantly in love. He tried explaining to me later how at that moment he became subsumed in a warm glow of domesticity and at last knew what he'd been seeking all his life: a little family of his own with Sherryn serving as saintly Madonna holding everyone steady in an unwavering orbit of kindness and love.

I tried explaining to Uncle Dirty that he'd apparently been imprinted like a baby duck, which tends to follow around the first moving object it sees after hatching, and wondered silently what component in my mix could have caused it. Maybe I was on the threshold of an important discovery. I told him he'd probably recover, but I needed more data. I suggested experiments in which Uncle Dirty dropped my caps in the presence of randomly selected women and let me note his reactions, but he wasn't interested and told me to go fuck myself.

Shortly afterward, and unrelated to that night, Sherryn and George had a serious argument, and George was kicked out. He seemed nonplussed, although because he was naturally quiet and passive and always stoned, even when climbing thirty-foot ladders in his bare feet while carrying buckets of paint, no emotion showed.

Uncle Dirty now began comforting Sherryn, an activity that usually ended in copulation. They fell in love and swore eternal fidelity. In his new state, Uncle Dirty shaved, got a haircut, took his clothes to a Laundromat, and went looking for a job on the mainland with the notion of supporting Sherryn and the kid. Then, as often happens, one of them fell out of love—Sherryn in this case. George was in California or Florida, I forget which. He and Sherryn were divorced by then, and Sherryn found a new guy who had real money, inspiring Uncle Dirty to return to the unemployment office—this time legally, because he'd actually been working for several months.

Just before Uncle Dirty fell for Sherryn there had been Cathy, a coed tossing them off the arm at the drugstore counter in Beach Haven. She was beyond gorgeous. Males of all ages lined up three-deep, jawing and pawing and panting and woofing, displaying every doggy behavior imaginable except pissing on the counter stools to mark their places. They represented the cream of the college crop, guys destined to be Wall Street tycoons, Ivy League lawyers, future surgeons to the President. Some of them had already arrived and were merely vacationing. Eighty-year-olds drooled while reprising distant memories not half as good. They were all just noise because if Cathy was in heat she didn't show it.

Then Uncle Dirty staggered in one night blasted on poppers and wearing his alert hair, eyes wide and brown as a startled buck's, heart barely tethered inside his chest from the amyl nitrate pumping through it. He said he couldn't afford the price of a cup of coffee, although he needed one badly, anything to ramp up the faltering rush. She told him her name was Cathy. He replied that he really didn't give a shit. She felt sorry for him and took a nickel from her own tips, punched it into the cash register, and poured him a cup. "Cream and sugar?" she'd asked. "I like my coffee the same as my women," he'd said. "Hot, black, and bitter. Too bad you're a bottle-blonde with medium-sized titties." This last was far from true.

Every other man had said he'd treat her like a princess, even promising immediate or future marriage, a life of ease and luxury smothered in mink. One guy offered to buy her a sports car on the spot, her choice of models, her color. Only Uncle Dirty, that special night, asked in his peculiar gentlemanly way if he might lick her pussy. Which he subsequently did with frightening regularity. And she proposed marriage to him, offering to accompany him into wrinkled old age, even to setting up housekeeping on the seat of his rusty Vespa and raising their children to be socialists.

Now Uncle Dirty yawned in her company, a sight she'd never experienced before. It drove her crazy. She began stalking him, showing up in our attic at odd hours and sitting politely while he honked and squawked on his tenor sax or looked bored and tried to explain why it was important for Coltrane's art that he be a junkie. He told her that here in America everyone was working hard, changing the culture to where women are respected as themselves.

Uncle Dirty and the rest of us hadn't noticed the invisible door through which we'd stepped into the fabulous sixties, into life as performance art, where the answers to humankind's big questions, Bob Dylan assured us, were blowin' in the wind. We were on the threshold of the Age of Aquarius, charter members of the Love Generation. Just around the corner were Woodstock, draft cards in flames, street protests against the Vietnam War, environmentalism's birth and the rise of feminism, the squalor of racism looming from TV screens as civil rights scrambled onto the national stage. Beside me is a grainy black and white photograph of Cap, Uncle Dirty, and me taken in September 1962. We stare down from the porch of the rooming house in the acedia of smug ignorance.

In April 2007, the three of us met at Key West for a final accounting. The forum was an open-air nude bar beside the sea. We rented a couple of shabby rooms nearby with toadstools growing in the showers and stayed arrantly drunk and stoned for a week, sharing morning joints with the giggling Haitian maids, themselves too stoned to clean our rooms.

Cap and I had not seen Uncle Dirty since the day of the photograph, and in the intervening years he'd devolved from young Beatnik into ancient Hippy. It seemed there wasn't a be-in he hadn't been in; the

Summer of Love had drained like dry sand through his fingers, just as every other summer before and since. He recalled being part of a crowd that sang protest songs and pelted New York City cops with daffodils, but couldn't tell us the purpose of the protest. Now his voice had attenuated to a thin whisper, and he coughed blood with every cigarette. The throat cancer killed him in July.

Cap served two tours in Viet Nam as an infantry officer and later contracted lung cancer. His own smoker's cough was accompanied by an enduring crepitation. After four decades he remained haunted by post-traumatic stress disorder and the recurring images of comrades forever youthful in death. He screamed nightly in his sleep. He told us that if real sleep is a state in which the conscious world drops away, then death is sleep without dreaming, a rich and infinite blackness. Cap died of respiratory failure in February 2010.

Of we three, only I remain to curate our intertwining memories. I can't tell you why. The answer is blowin' in the wind.

# *Blacking Out*

I HAD BEEN BLACKING OUT regularly since coming back to college. During these episodes I would be simultaneously awake and unconscious, splendidly drunk but still able to function. If by functioning you mean walking around doing and saying stupid things.

A psychologist might have diagnosed an inability to deal with certain issues, something I considered too, except that the issues, whatever they were, remained distant and out of focus. It seemed simpler to sit at a bar clutching a glass slick with condensation, a soggy pack of smokes at hand, and not think about anything. Eventually the night—the real night—would arrive like a train stuttering and shrieking along tracks laid too far apart. Then nothing mattered.

It was common to wake up on the floor of someone's grimy apartment not remembering how I got there. The occupant was usually a guy no longer in school but with whom I had taken classes, a vestigial presence on the fringes peering in, still wearing a thin patina of hope.

A few of these acquaintances, dimly recalled even then, were flame-outs from the pre-med program. Medical school had appeared to them as a collage of tattered images, mostly themselves wearing sterile white jackets stuffed with cash, driving sports cars, an adoring nurse blowing into each ear, but rarely anything associated with saving lives. In better days they gathered in the Student Union and talked about the MCAT, jacking up their group prospects by thinking if you scored high enough a dean from Harvard Med would come groveling, holding an invitation to join its freshman class despite the awful grades, jerky amphetamine bounce, and fingers stained brown with nicotine. They discussed it until talk morphed into a suitable substitute for achievement. Why hit the books when you can coast until test day? Then they were gone.

It was all boring as hell. No one was paying attention to whether I personally attended classes, myself included. The grades were not good. I was skipping lectures and labs and about to tumble down the worn marble steps of conventional knowledge pursued by unread textbooks flapping like haunted crows.

I'd taken time away from school to work on boats in the Caribbean, kicking aimlessly through islands known only from maps, meeting people just like me—not lost exactly, but unlikely to be found either. It was now the winter of '61 or '62. The sky above my side of the Ohio River was ugly and bleeding snow. I was a biology major, not pre-med, and musing about how after so much time in the sun I was building up colecalciferol reserves and stockpiling vitamin D3. The thought was comforting, if inadequate to stifle the constant urge to jump off a bridge.

Sometimes on restless nights I walked to the middle of the Sixth Street Bridge just to stare down at the brown water of the Ohio and trace its serpentine eddies under moonlight. I felt neither fear nor a specific desire to kill myself; the urge was simply to jump and tumble freely through the air; to pull loose from all attachments by leaping the rail and sinking underneath the currents; to float weightless and unencumbered.

At such times I remembered the Caribbean and how sunbeams drill through the clouds that collect over tropical oceanic islands, gathering in broad ropes above the sea's surface as if inviting you to climb them. A grizzled Cruzan had told me that's how you could find God, by shinnying up a sunbeam past the clouds into heaven. No different, he said, than climbing a coconut palm, just a bigger reward at the top. Then he laughed and his face collapsed in a moonscape of wrinkles.

I was sitting at a bar on the corner of Third Avenue and nowhere, admiring its miasmic stench and skunk-town blues. This was in Huntington, the state's biggest metropolis, population then about a hundred thousand. Later the C & O Railroad would move its offices elsewhere and twenty thousand would emigrate, leaving streets fronted by rotting houses.

Monk and two of our cronies from the coal camp near a town where I briefly attended high school had driven eighty miles to track me down, having heard I was back. I knew the mines weren't hiring, that their real motivation was boredom. No one had a job except Monk, who was in the Marines. His job was killing people. He, too, became unemployed in '66, when a VC sniper shot him as he waded among rice.

At some point, everybody decided to chip in and buy me a ten-dollar hooker upstairs as a welcome home present. I took their money, a pathetic pile of coins and crumpled dollar bills, and climbed the narrow stairs beside the men's room. At the top was a large man without any front teeth. "Seven bucks," he said. I counted out seven and pocketed the difference.

The room was confining, cluttered, the wallpaper looking like the aftereffects of a bad sunburn. The only illumination came from a low-watt bulb in a lamp atop a dresser. The light was further dimmed by a pair of panties tossed carelessly over the shade.

The girl, in the bed with a sheet pulled up to her neck, acted nervous. She was straight from the camps, with thin scraggly hair, possibly sixteen or seventeen. I must have been about nineteen. She looked into my burned-out eyes, noticed the hair hanging uncut for a year, the thick black beard, the face tanned chestnut-brown. I was nearly six feet tall but had returned thin enough to hide inside my shadow.

"You ain't one of them freaks, are you?" she said. "Because if you are, all I got to do is pull this here rope. It's got a bell on the end, and Cedric will come busting in and put a hurt on you."

I thought to practice some Spanish. "No problemo," I said. "It's just invisible old me, strange but harmless."

As I was leaving, Cedric offered two Quaaludes for three bucks, a steep price in places other than here in the Bible Belt, where illegal drugs were rare as rubies on a playground. I'd learned from summers lifeguarding at the Jersey shore how 'ludes washed down with boilermakers can fluff up the rushing darkness and make it stand taller. I handed over the rest of the money without guilt. The guys needed gas for the drive home, but I knew Junebug always carried an empty gas can and a siphon hose in his trunk. An untended vehicle parked on a dark street was easy to find.

When I got back to the bar Uncle Dirty whispered, "I can tell you're holding. Give." I felt his hand bumping my thigh under the table. I slipped a 'lude in his palm, which he expertly popped into his mouth while pretending to wipe his hand across his face. Uncle Dirty didn't know my friends. He'd tagged along to West Virginia because he had nowhere else to go. Nowhere urgent, anyway. He'd been there for the latter part of my Caribbean stay and was now scrounging bus fare back to New York and a job as dishwasher at a Greenwich Village coffee house. "What was it?" he asked.

"What was what?"

"What I just ate, dipshit."

I told him. Then Monk, who possessed exceptional paranoia blended with pathological aggressiveness, offered up the inevitable: "Why's this guy whispering?"

"He tends to choke on his own horseshit," I said.

"Well, hell, that makes sense," Monk said. "I do it myself sometimes." We all laughed.

In a few months this nighttime routine would break along with the weather.

AN ISOLATED POND ON A warm, windless night retains a hidden restiveness. I liked sitting on a damp bank surrounded by creaks, groans, peeps, belches, grunts, and the reassuring whine of mosquitoes, awash in froggish comfort.

Even better was shucking my clothes, pulling on a mask and snorkel, and slipping under the surface holding a watertight flashlight. The pond I often went to was shallow, not more than a dozen feet deep. To my knowledge, I was its only human visitor. I entered barefoot so as not to dislodge the near-weightless layer of detritus covering every object. The secret to keeping good visibility was moving as little as possible. Flippers would have been detrimental. No arm-flailing, just feeble hand strokes; no kicking, just breath control to sink and rise.

Descent through a surface layer of duckweed into a gloomy forest of pondweeds, then to an understory of epibenthic algae. Finally a substratum of sullen muck littered with branches, logs, stumps; the occasional boulder rising abruptly like a frozen shoulder. Inert objects and weeds rushed forward—jabbing, grasping, looming—yet my risk of drowning by entanglement was no greater than for any other amphibious creature. We were naked, skins slippery, evolutionary adaptations infallible.

In spring the subsurface vista was draped in necklaces of frogspawn, their gelatinous beads alive with pulsating embryos. As temperatures increased, crowds of bream hovered in the water column, light-struck and motionless, those in the distance ghostly outlines revealed by their eyeshine. An occasional bass drifted through them, a cat among mice, waiting for dawn. Sometimes a water snake or eel twisted in and out of view following the bottom contour. Foraging crayfish flipped away from my beam in reverse, seeking darkness. A turtle stirred in sleepy confusion before scurrying under a log, leaving behind a puff of mud. Everywhere, creeping snails.

Gravity disappeared in this viscous place. I could soar, hover, and land simply by holding or expelling air—just another particle among the plankton and fish jizzum. Through the surface I saw the moon shatter and reassemble itself over and over. Water pressing against my eardrums formed an unbroken acoustic near-field through which every sound became magnified, its place of origin indeterminate, until the faintest noise could no longer be distinguished from the pond itself.

I was there to revel in the roiled juices and gain a silent knowledge modulated in terrestrial company by drink, drugs, and pussy. And I vowed never to let up on the accelerator. Not until that turning moment when the blackness closes over and I run aground on some desiccated shore.

# *Parking Sharks*

In August 2013, a shark was found on the floor of a New York City subway car. It was on the N train bound for Queens and first reported as having been seen at the 14th Street stop. The species was never identified, but the photo indicates to me that it was a member of a group called the dogfishes. This one looked about a foot long and maybe two pounds.

Why bring up such a minor event? Only because in June of '66 Win and I left a dead shark in the parking lot of a truck stop outside Rochester, New York. It was a different species than the subway specimen. Ours had been a sandbar shark of seven feet and perhaps a hundred pounds. I ought to know. I was the guy who lifted it out of its transport tank and kicked it onto the pavement so its decomposing body wouldn't foul the water and kill the rest of our specimens riding with it.

To my knowledge, this shark never made the news, but I've often wondered what people leaving the diner on their way west must have thought. I mean, there it was lying dead and fully on display that summer afternoon, smelling terrible and taking up its own parking space.

We were on the way back to the Aquarium of Niagara Falls with a load of specimens pulled out of a commercial pound net off Point Judith, Rhode Island. Win was director of the aquarium; I was its curator. Win had recently bought a huge trailer from a traveling circus that was folding. It contained two built-in fiberglass tanks that each held eight thousand gallons and several smaller ones of about a thousand gallons. He and I and the aquarium maintenance crew had rewired the inside and installed a gasoline generator to power air compressors, circulating and transfer pumps, and lights. We devised floating hatch covers made of waterproofed, full-sized doors like you install in houses, to minimize slosh from the big tanks, although any water that slopped over ran into scuppers on the floor and collected in sumps where submersible pumps directed it back in a loop.

Now that we had the equipment to transport large specimens we needed a way of getting it to the collection sites and back. Neither Win nor I had ever driven an eighteen-wheeler, but Win said it couldn't be that hard.

We rented the cab and hired a licensed trucker to hook up the trailer and drive the rig out to a truck stop on the New York State Thruway where he showed us how to shift gears, back up, park, hitch and unhitch the trailer, and so forth. Win and I took turns practicing for a couple of hours, then our instructor's buddy came to pick him up and we set off back to the aquarium, pulling off to the side once to switch seats. The ride was harrowing, but it came with a thrilling sense of power, as if we'd been suddenly blessed by the reeking gods of diesel and melting macadam. Win even rolled the window down and yelled, "Get out of the way, pissants!" As I said, this was in June '66 when Win was forty-five and I was twenty-four.

The physiology of sharks was only just starting to be understood in the sixties. Dogma in the public aquarium trade posited that keeping sharks alive during transport required pumping pure bottled oxygen across their submerged gills. However, doing this makes the water hyperoxic, raising the dissolved oxygen concentration far above normal.

When humans hold their breath, lactic acid accumulates in the blood, rendering it slightly acidic and triggering the autonomic breathing response, which is nearly instantaneous. A fish or shark's response is far slower because water is more than seven hundred times denser than air. Transport of gases and their reaction products is by diffusion and ion exchange at the gill surfaces, and the autonomic response is controlled not by the accumulation of blood carbon dioxide and subsequent acidosis, as in mammals, but by the concentration of oxygen in the surrounding water.

Immersing a shark in seawater containing excessive oxygen reduces its breathing rate, even to the point of stopping it completely. Stated differently, when seawater contains too much oxygen, a shark has no physiological "reason" to breathe, the consequences being that it "forgets" and dies of acidosis despite a surfeit of oxygen available to its gills.

Articles describing the physiology of this process, learned in laboratories from testing captive sharks, were being published in the journal *Respiration Physiology* by a team of French scientists, and I was reading them avidly. Win and I discussed these novel findings, but he was busy with administrative duties requiring him to wear a necktie and attend lots of meetings. "Bureaucratic bullshit," he called it. He told me to work out the practical aspects of an alternative to the oxygen-infusion method of transport, that we needed some sharks on exhibit because the ones we'd caught in Rhode Island had died on the way back or shortly thereafter.

Win loathed sitting behind his desk. What he liked was scuba diving for live specimens or fishing for them. Anything to get to sea, and he created opportunities to make sure it happened.

A couple of weeks after the Rhode Island trip he telephoned Frank, his brother-in-law in Ocean City, New Jersey. Rosemarie was Win's wife, and Frank was married to Rosemarie's sister, whose name I forget. Frank said to come down, that we could use his new twenty-six-foot Chris Craft to catch sharks. This was also a chance for Rosemarie to visit her sister. Rosemarie had three young sons from a previous marriage. I don't recall their ages, but probably between five and ten.

Rosemarie and her kids drove down in the family car, taking along my first wife Judith and our daughter Sara. We were to stay at Frank's, who said he had plenty of room. Win and I rented a cab and hauled down the trailer with our collecting gear.

We stashed the rig in the parking lot of the marina where Frank kept his boat. The first night I started the generator and pumped the tanks full of seawater using the big self-priming transfer pump, then got the lights, circulation pumps, and air compressor going.

I soon saw that Frank was in the final stages of cirrhotic breakdown. His sclera and skin were jaundiced. His ankles had ballooned and turned black to the point he could no longer wear shoes; his abdomen looked like he'd swallowed a basketball. He came across as a nice, gentle guy, if sometimes incoherent.

Frank assured us he'd sworn off the hard stuff and weaned himself to a daily case of beer and a ration of paregoric. To Win that seemed a reasonable compromise. "You should have seen the sonuvabitch before," he told me. "Jesus Christ, we used to go fishing in his old boat—the one before this new one—and Frank would down a fifth of bourbon in a couple of hours. Nothing to it. And he never stumbled or fell, just stood there rooted to the deck like a tree no matter how rough it got. Fucking amazing."

Frank was fixated on his new washing machine and took every opportunity to show anyone nearby how it worked and how cool it was. He was always dropping something into it like a mother bird feeding its open-mouthed baby. A single shirt or pair of underwear sufficed, or a swimsuit—whatever was around. Anything to keep it churning. It had a glass door on the front, and I guess Frank was mesmerized by watching his laundry flip over.

We'd brought along eighteen Danforth anchors, each weighing fifteen pounds. I'd rigged them with six feet of chain held to the shanks with turnbuckles. The flukes would dig into the sandy bottom, providing strength sufficient to hold a modest-sized boat in place on a rough sea. Win figured they ought to retain any sharks we hooked. The ends of the chains were connected with eye splices to seventy-five-foot lengths of stout polypropylene line. I'd spent evenings making those splices, braiding each over a galvanized thimble, and they could have withstood an elephant's pull. At the other end of every line was a Styrofoam buoy. The fishhooks were rigged with chain leaders and turnbuckles, so if a hooked shark started to spin while trying to escape, it was less likely to become entangled in the buoy line.

For bait we had several boxes of frozen mackerel thawing slowly on ice in the trailer. Late the next afternoon Win, Frank, and I motored out of the marina and through the channel to the open ocean. Once well beyond the surf we baited all the hooks and tossed the rigs overboard. Win's plan was to let the bait "soak" overnight.

Early the next morning we went out to check them. We'd caught a half-dozen or so sharks that were still alive, sandbars and lemons, all within sight of the public beach, and all too big to lift onto the deck and wrestle into our portable transport tank. Others had been hooked but died struggling to escape. To save ourselves some nasty bites recovering the gear, Win shot the live ones in the head with a .22 pistol.

Leaving the bait out overnight was obviously too long. We needed to catch the sharks more quickly and get them back to the truck in livelier condition. We also preferred specimens less than about seven feet long. We returned to the dock and made a new plan. The sharks we hoped to catch feed most consistently at twilight, defined in biology as dawn and dusk. Win decided to wait until evening to drop the bait overboard, hang around at sea three hours or so, and then lift them after dark, presumably when the sharks had already fed.

Rosemarie's kids wanted to come along, so when supper was over we set out again. Frank was in no condition to help, but he came too. Win drove the boat and I served as mate. I started putting a whole mackerel on each hook after we left the dock, and everything was ready by the time Win found a location he liked, at which point the two of us started setting out the bait. Then we waited.

With darkness came a fierce storm from the northeast accompanied by thunder and lightning, and the sea suddenly blew up. I rummaged around underneath the seats while Win held the boat into the wind. There were four life jackets aboard; I put them on Frank and the kids.

Picking up the lines was out of the question, so we started for the marina. The channel entrance was marked by two reflective can buoys, but the rain was coming sideways, and the swells were now several feet tall with angry white heads. Our original compass bearings were of little use in finding the channel because we had motored both north and south looking for the entrance and knew only it was somewhere to the west. I asked Win about calling the Coast Guard on the radio, but he figured we didn't need the help, at least not yet. What we needed was light.

By now the sea was breaking violently over the deck. We got Frank to take the kids below and stay there with them. I took a flashlight and crawled out onto the raised foredeck. The wind-driven rain mixed with sea spray carried such a sting that I could barely open my eyes. I felt water pummeling me from all directions and the boat bucking and slamming into the swells. I flattened out on my stomach, arms and legs spread wide, trying to brace myself on the slick fiberglass surface, hoping my feeble beam would bounce off one of the buoys and show the way back.

Behind me in the cabin Win had the wipers going, but they were useless against the volume of water hitting us. He said later he only noticed I'd been pitched overboard when the light disappeared. "You were there, and then you weren't," he said. "It was funny as hell." There was no use looking for me in the blackness, and Frank would obviously have been no help.

He'd been pretty loaded even before leaving the dock and nipping on his bottle of paregoric ever since.

I hit the water and immediately kicked off the tennis shoes, which served no purpose in that situation. I was wearing thin chinos and a T-shirt. I shed the pants, zipped them back up, and tied a knot in each ankle. While treading water, I spread apart the waistband. I held the waist open and flung the pants over my head and underwater, trapping air in the legs. I cinched the waist, held it in one fist, and stuck my neck between the inflated legs. The pants became a makeshift life jacket, allowing me to float several minutes at a time without struggling, until the waves pounded out the air and the process had to be repeated.

I wasn't wearing a watch and couldn't have seen its face anyway. Win didn't note the time when I disappeared over the side, but I was probably treading out there about three hours. The storm abated gradually, and the whitecaps started settling down.

Eventually only huge swells remained. I continued to ride them, dipping into the deep troughs and being lifted to the crests, but mostly not changing location, the water molecules under me turning in stationary circles of descending size as ocean waves are known to do. In a stormy sea it isn't the waves that travel, but rather the disturbance. The motion is inexhaustible; it's you who becomes exhausted while not going anywhere.

The sky cleared enough that I could see the lights of Ocean City far in the distance, little more than a glow on the horizon. I was drifting slowly seaward and beginning to shiver. *What the hell,* I thought, and started swimming toward the glow, taking note which direction the swells were moving so as not to become disoriented when dropped into the troughs.

Exactly how much time passed is impossible to say, but there was a brightness that wasn't lightning. I started yelling and waving my arms, and a blinding light suddenly washed over my face. A Coast Guard vessel came alongside; hands plucked me out of the water and onto the deck. Someone draped a blanket across my shoulders and asked how I was. I said I was fine. The Coasties told me Win had radioed and explained my situation, that they'd found Frank's boat with everyone okay. It was waiting at the channel entrance. They dropped me off.

The first thing Win said was, "Did you think you were going to drown?"

"No," I told him truthfully.

He laughed. "I did." He also mentioned that it's usually a bad idea to go for a night swim on top of baited shark lines.

The next afternoon we went out again, picked up what gear we could find, and reset the baits. We continued to catch a few sharks each trip over the next several days, some of them huge. Once we hauled up a hook with just a head attached. The rest of the shark had been bitten off in what appeared to be just one or two bites. We estimated the head to weigh at least fifty pounds.

We also caught some specimens of perfect size for exhibition. They all made it back to the aquarium alive.

A couple of weeks later Win got a call at work from Rosemarie saying Frank had collapsed and died on his laundry-room floor. Win beckoned me into his office, shut the door, and took out the bottle of bourbon from his bottom desk drawer. We poured ourselves a couple and mused whether Frank's last image was his skivvies turning somersaults.

At the dock that night after the storm there had been tears in his eyes. He'd hugged me and kept repeating how happy he was to still be alive. He was saying in his hoarse whisper, "We made it! We fucking made it!"

# *Key Largo*

I ALWAYS DRIFT CLOSE TO water during those times of the unrelieved sorries when the world is yanking me sideways. Poking around in it slows the heart and drains away hopeless thoughts. I feel an easy quiet when examining a patch of wetness for evidence of life—whether it's an ocean or bayou, a flooded tire track or tiny Appalachian creek—as if reaffirming my own.

On one occasion, such a place was Molasses Reef three miles out in the Atlantic off Key Largo, Florida. On a particular summer night in the early 1970s this was, for me, a source of wide and mysterious wonder. The timing was perfect because I had a decision to make.

But first, a prelude. I was living at Key Largo, having resigned as director of Aquarium of Niagara Falls to take a breather. I wanted to spend as much time as possible underwater studying marine life. One way of doing this was to work on a dive boat, which also provided income. The captain's name was Frank, a friend originally from Buffalo and a former Navy SEAL. We were running a boat taking scuba divers out to the reefs in John Pennekamp Coral Reef State Park to fish watch. Among my duties as mate was helping the divers into their gear, getting them safely to the bottom, and babysitting the group during a slow tour of the reefs while the dive boat stayed tied to a mooring buoy. A deckhand named Tyrone was usually along to help, but he and Frank were topside while everyone else was underwater.

Tyrone had been an Army Ranger in Vietnam. He was a Seminole Indian born and raised in the Everglades who wore shades night and day and rarely spoke. He also walked around with four-pound dive weights strapped to his ankles "for power." Tyrone, like Frank, was potentially a very bad dude, but Frank was usually isolated in the wheelhouse. Tyrone's unconventional appearance and manner often invited ridicule. I always made a point of warning the macho-type divers with loud mouths to leave him alone. One guy said, "That skinny shit? What's he gonna to do, kill me?" I told him that it was a possibility. Luckily, confrontations were avoided.

We worked for a guy named Carl, a former Marine officer who owned a dive shop near the park entrance. He taught scuba lessons, sold and rented dive equipment, and owned two boats that ferried people out to the reefs twice daily for their dives. The smaller vessel was the Henrietta, the larger a beamy fifty-footer named *Reef Queen.* Frank, Tyrone, and I usually worked aboard her.

A half-day trip cost ten dollars a person and included two dives, and the *Queen* was licensed to carry twenty-five passengers. We left the dock at nine o'clock in the morning and made the half-hour run to the reefs three miles offshore. There were several potential sites within the park's boundaries, all marked with mooring buoys. Their function was to encourage boaters to tie off *To The Mooring Buoys!* instead of tossing anchors overboard and damaging the corals. Those we visited depended on Frank's assessment of the weather, sea conditions, and whether another vessel hadn't tied off first. Some sites were shallow, twelve feet or so, others thirty to fifty-five feet.

At the end of the first dive we got everyone aboard, switched to fresh tanks, and moved to another location. Afterward we returned to the dock. We then repeated the process, departing for the afternoon dives at one thirty.

Tyrone and I generally got to the shop at seven-thirty and assembled the gear, including two scuba tanks and weight belts for each prepaid guest and two tanks for me. We checked each tank's air pressure, loaded everything into one of Carl's vans, drove the mile or so to the dock, and lugged the stuff aboard the *Queen*. At lunchtime we took back the empty tanks to be filled by someone else and returned with full ones, after again checking the pressure in each. At the end of the day we hauled everything back to the dive shop before cleaning up the boat, coiling the lines, swiping out the heads and areas below deck, and stowing everything in its designated place. At least one guest had usually barfed on the deck during the afternoon trip. Morning barfs got hosed into the scuppers during noon break.

I'd hoped to have time for personal fish watching on these excursions, but that seldom happened. Carl was focused on income, which made him disinclined to check certification cards. People routinely lied, telling him they were experienced divers when the closest they might have come to being underwater, at least in Florida, was standing in a motel shower. My time was consumed watching up to twenty-five divers at a time and attempting to predict which of them might panic just from having his head submerged or suck up an hour's worth of air in fifteen minutes and then panic. Because we were always careful to weight each person properly, once the group submerged it was easy to distinguish the novices, those who hyperventilated and flailed around even when neutrally buoyant.

I was always inflating people's life vests, following them to the surface, and shoving them close to the dive platform where Frank and Tyrone could drag them aboard coughing up seawater and puking and shaking with anxiety. In rough weather the bottom surge caused people to become seasick and throw up in their regulators, which in turn caused them to inhale or swallow seawater and become disoriented. I watched more than a few forget the advice to always swim against a current and start drifting off into the great blue Atlantic.

The *Reef Queen* herself was a detriment to comfort and safety, wallowing sickeningly during calm conditions and yawing violently when the sea blew up, at which time the crew scrambled to secure the gear, especially any scuba tanks not stowed in the racks. Left to roll around in the open, they were liable to shift and injure someone. The combined odors of vomit and bilge water in the heads below deck were enough to make even a seasoned sailor queasy.

Then there was the hassle and hazard of getting people aboard while the dive platform slammed up and down in the swells, threatening to crush the skulls of surfacing divers. The job, to my dismay, was actually more stressful than the one I had just quit.

A retired Army vet everyone called Sarge owned a bar and restaurant situated back in the mangroves off a barely passable one-lane track covered in crushed coral rock. At the end of the day, most of us in the dive business went there for an attitude adjustment. The parking lot, also covered in crushed coral, flooded at high tide, and anyone who parked too close to the mangroves ended up wading to his car at closing time.

The place was neither large nor small. A single bulb illuminated the rickety wooden porch teetering unevenly on low pilings where a sign beside the entrance said SARGE's. Sarge never advertised, but on Friday evenings starting at five o'clock it was all-you-can-eat fried grouper and French fries for a buck and a quarter and draft beer at half price. As night came on, the big tarpon in the lagoon out front started jumping and smacking the water with their sides, and the warm wind diminished to a whisper. Lizards slipped into their sleepy-time cracks in the walls; tree frogs and katydids competed with the jukebox's shit-kicker music. From sea level, you couldn't get any closer to heaven.

Then one day Sarge's worst nightmare came true: his place was "discovered" by the restaurant reviewer of a big Miami newspaper. She wrote about its charm, the great food (if you didn't mind everything fried) and cheap drinks, and her article was accompanied by a little map showing its location off the Overseas

Highway. Within days Sarge's was overrun with outsiders, many accompanied by children and even dogs. They wanted to know if the stuffed water moccasin behind the bar was still alive, whether the ratty stuffed gator just inside the front door had eaten anyone lately. They gaped at yellowed mounts of local gamefishes, themselves bright-eyed and gaping and now gripping the unpainted walls in terrestrial stasis. They reported that the bathrooms stank while also noting the conspicuous absence of toilet paper. Those expecting proper hygiene to go with their Florida cracker dining experience told Sarge as much, and he mostly told them to go to hell.

This new scene had a depressing effect on Sarge's two waitresses, now forced to accelerate beyond their usual slow shuffle. Their complaining and use of foul language escalated until one quit and the other asked that her hours be cut. Finally, in a fit of smug anger, a rage destitute in its insignificance, Sarge removed the window screens and invited every mosquito and noseeum within shouting distance to come inside and enjoy the hospitality. He took a ball-peen hammer to the breaker switch that turned his ceiling fans in wobbling circles like deranged moths. He muttered to himself, take that, sumbitches, and to those who still remained at the bar, either unperturbed by biting insects or too drunk to notice them, he said, "Take that, goddammit!" Once again, his clientele had been reduced to the loyal few coming and going in alcoholic confusion and righteous poverty. This pleased him, and he started smiling again. I knew I'd miss this place and everything else.

Decision time arrived. I was off the next day, so instead of heading to Sarge's after work I took a full scuba tank and regulator from the dive shop and tossed them in the pickup. I bought a couple of bottles of water and two sandwiches at the snack shop in the Park and stuffed them in a knapsack. After telling Frank my intentions so he'd come looking for me if I didn't make it back, I borrowed one of the Park's rental boats with a full load of gas and headed out to sea. My wife already knew the plan and wasn't expecting me home that night.

It was nearly sunset when I tied off on the vacant buoy above Molasses Reef. The surface was calm with just a few cat paws ruffling the surface, the eastern sky still holding its leftovers of vacant blue. Winter had arrived, and a cold front up north had drifted down to us. With darkness, the day's residual warmth abruptly vanished.

I fumbled in the dark putting new batteries in the underwater flashlight and waited for moonrise, then leaned back and considered the choices. I'd been offered the job of curator at the New England Aquarium in Boston and a similar position at the New

York Aquarium and Osborn Laboratories of Marine Sciences in the Coney Island section of Brooklyn. Which to choose?

Weather conditions stayed calm and pleasant, and about eleven o'clock I dropped a tab of acid, struggled into the scuba gear, put on my mask, snorkel, and flippers and sat through the brief interval of retching over the side. Then I turned on the flashlight and rolled overboard. I drifted toward the bottom in parallel with the buoy line to where it was anchored permanently at about thirty feet and settled cross-legged on a patch of white sand. The reef loomed up on all sides. I started to skip-breathe, inhaling and exhaling slowly, basically skipping alternate breaths to make the air last longer. By sucking this way on one of Carl's big tanks, I'd last nearly two hours before needing to surface.

The acid reconfigured the world in a rush. Suddenly I was trapped inside a wind tunnel or enmeshed in the spiraling folds of a waterspout. The sound of my bubbles grew louder as they collided and coalesced. I switched off the flashlight and looked up, seeing them flash silver against the downwelling moonlight. The noise was terrifying and out of synchrony, like the Doppler effect from a fast-moving train. I turned the flashlight on and tried to focus it horizontally, but the beam dragged along a ghostly tracing each time my arm moved, or was the previous location only an advent of its future placement? The light, too, seemed out of synchrony. By now the effect had hit fully, and I'd attained anoesis. The visual world was a kaleidoscope of eidetic images.

A green moray eel emerged from the base of the reef and undulated toward me, opening and closing its mouth rhythmically as it breathed. Suddenly it turned inside itself, intestines glowing impossibly red, liver quivering and purple and unfolding in slow motion, morphing into the expanded corolla of a Japanese iris. Zooplankton, attracted to the light beam, swirled insanely, eyes glowing iridescent red and orange. The reef itself opened, fractured, conflated, then rose and drifted overhead in a diaphanous cloud.

I lay on my stomach and inched forward until eye-level with the corals. In a crevice a parrotfish slept its lidless sleep encased in a nighttime cocoon of mucus, nocturnal colors vibrant and pulsating. I could detect each individual cell of its skin, see pigments flowing like dark lava inside the microscopic chromatophores. A spiny lobster, huge and alien, backed farther into the reef. Coral polyps expanded and rippled in the weak current, changing size and staring out of grotesque, eyeless faces.

I entered a synesthesia of sorts, movements synchronized to a primal melody in time with the driving metronome of my exhalations. I could taste each flashing color. The lobster emerged, dactyls scissoring as it picked some edible particle off the sand. It wiggled its eyestalks and waved its antennae, attempting to determine my identity. Time passed. I didn't know how much time, but eventually breathing became difficult as the air supply dwindled. I reached back and pulled the reserve. Another fifteen minutes. The rushing in my ears subsided, the world was turning calm. I found the buoy line, switched off the flashlight, and ascended slowly, following the bubbles.

I surfaced beside the boat, grabbed the gunwale, hoisted up, and rolled aboard. Black clouds peppered the moon, causing it to disappear intermittently, and the air felt cold. I peeled away the gear, dried off, and lay back on the center seat. The acid trip lasted another couple of hours, but I'd discovered what I needed to know: Boston would be too boring. I pulled the towel over me and slept.

# *Coney Island*

I KNEW AS SOON AS we got to the parking lot and saw the back window of our car busted out and all our stuff gone that moving to Brooklyn might not have been one of my best decisions.

I'd accepted the job as curator of the New York Aquarium and Osborn Laboratories of Marine Sciences at Coney Island. This was in January of '71, I think. My second wife, Carol, and I had driven up from Key Largo, Florida, where we'd lived for several months while I took a breather from actual work and helped run a boat taking scuba divers out to the reefs at John Pennekamp Coral Reef State Park. It had felt right, getting back in the water several times a day to watch fishes, and the sun had felt good too. Now I needed to put my career back on track, which meant getting a real job.

We'd found a cheap motel in Coney Island. It seemed to have rooms you could rent by the night instead of by the hour. In front was an illuminated sign advertising secure parking. I remember asking the clerk if the lot really was secure. He'd shrugged and said it was secure as things got around here. He'd said it without actually lifting his head and looking at me. So we took the room and the next morning everything we owned not packed in the suitcases we took inside was gone.

A cop from the 60th precinct came by to take our statement. He yawned frequently. "What'd youse lose?" I told him: a stereo, dive equipment, clothes, books, the usual stuff people take along when they move. He tapped his pen on his clipboard and sucked his teeth. "Junkies," he said. "Fuhgetaboutit."

We drove to Queens and stayed with a guy we knew and started looking for a place to live. The guy was a pilot with Eastern Airlines based out of LaGuardia. We had the place pretty much to ourselves. Our host spent his off days with his wife and son at their house in New Hampshire and was hardly ever in Queens except to shower and change into his uniform and maybe flop on the couch for a night.

My new associates at work advised living on Staten Island or Long Island, saying that Coney Island was too dangerous, for kids especially, neighborhoods near the beach in particular. I wanted to be close to work and disliked the thought of commuting. Carol and I didn't have children together, and my two kids were living with my first wife and her second husband in Newberg, New York, on the Hudson River.

Carol started checking out rentals in Coney Island. There was a high-rise at Brighton First Road and Boardwalk a few blocks from the aquarium and labs, but the rental agent said she had a dozen people or more waiting for the single vacancy, a nice corner two-bedroom unit on the seventh floor with a balcony and full view of Coney Island Beach.

Carol had been a flight attendant and knew how to talk to people. A couple of nights later the agent called. When I answered the phone she said the place was ours. I asked how that happened, how we could have jumped to the head of the line, and the woman told me it was because Carol had been the only prospective renter within her personal living memory who had treated her politely and with respect. According to her, people from Brooklyn behave like assholes, and that we'd soon find this out.

Getting to work was simple: elevator to the ground floor, out the door, up a few steps to the boardwalk, and a fifteen-minute walk to the aquarium's side entrance. That short stroll provided interesting distractions. Back then the Brighton Beach section of Coney Island was Jewish, many of the inhabitants aging immigrants from Eastern Europe who had come over after World War II. They commandeered the boardwalk benches in fair weather and foul, speaking Yiddish. I once asked an old Polish guy who lived in our building what they talked about all day. "They don't talk," he said. "They complain."

Some sat with eyes closed, faces tilted up to capture whatever meager photons fell from the winter sky. Others read or played chess or cribbage. But the boardwalk was a smorgasbord of humanity. Even at sunrise you'd see lovers, junkies, dope dealers, venders, joggers, bikers, panhandlers, crazed poets, whores, guys offering discreet blowjobs, and other people who looked ordinary and were just walking around dazed. Homeless people living in permanent camps underneath the boardwalk emerged blinking like moles and kicking the sand for lost change or something they could hock or sell. Muggers and pickpockets skulked around the food and beer stands hoping for the daylight to end quickly and night to arrive.

I sometimes took side trips, self-guided tours of the subterranean. It was not at all like a coalmine down there with the footsteps overhead sometimes dampened by rain or snow. Odors of piss and puke; green bottles of dago red passed hand to hand, and junkies shooting up. Furtive blowjobs among the pilings and scattered trash. Displays of pussy and dicks and assholes available to buy, rent, or merely inspect. Glue for sale, your own pastrami-tainted lunch bag suitable for huffing. A supererogatory shopper's delight, Walmart with a sand floor and attentive muggers standing by to roll you a cart. *Hey stranger! Yeah, you motherfucker. Got a cig?*

At the bottom of every set of stairs from the boardwalk to the beach was a flasher, naked except for his shoes and trench coat. Competition was fierce for locations with the highest pedestrian traffic, and I once watched two guys duke it out over a particularly choice spot. They rolled in the sand punching each other ineffectually. The smaller guy eventually ran away. The winner then took off his coat. He stood nude, holding it up with one hand and brushing vigorously with the other, taking care after putting it back on to be certain the collar was properly squared away.

One denizen of this bizarre ecosystem was a female flasher everyone called Crazy Lil. She was dirty and frazzled and strode rapidly along, head down and muttering, wrapped in her own arms like an octopus. Summer and winter she wore only men's work boots and a ratty trench coat and performed on the boardwalk itself, not at the bottom of the stairs like the men who flashed and ducked out of sight into the darkness. She'd walk up to you shouting, "I know what you men want! Well, here it is! Come and git it!" And she'd fling open her coat while forcing her insane empty eyes on you and laughing hysterically out of a toothless mouth.

Then there was the little homeless guy who frequented Nathan's. You had to keep a close eye on your hot dog when he was around. He didn't exactly steal hot dogs; he stole bites out of them. I watched him one summer day making his noon rounds. The boardwalk in front of Nathan's was packed with people talking and laughing and eating, not paying attention. He'd sidle up beside a customer, take a quick bite out of his dog, and put it back on the paper plate without the victim being aware of what happened. He moved to other tables, repeating the process, sometimes even stealing a sip of someone's Coke through the straw without touching the cup.

Security guards patrolling inside the aquarium were always on the lookout for Willie the Feeler. He was a normal-looking guy dressed in normal-looking clothes. The main exhibit hall was dark, the only illumination coming from dim footlights and light spilling out through the front glass panels of the exhibits. Willie enjoyed feeling up women and quickly disappearing into the crowd. The guards would hear surprised squeals and start hunting Willie down so they could toss him out. Willie obviously wasn't hurting for money because he always seemed to have the price of admission. I advised the ticket sellers and ticket takers to be on the alert and stop him at the entrance, but they were too busy, and he was too nondescript.

One time the guards reported it was Willie's screams they heard. After Willie had grabbed a woman's ass she'd turned with the speed of an enraged leopard, wrestled him to the floor, and clubbed him repeatedly with her handbag. When the guards arrived, she was pounding Willie like a gristled sirloin and yelling, "Take that, you goddamn pervert!" Cops from the 60th were called, but the victim was a visitor from out of town and declined to press charges, thinking, I guess, she might have to come back and go to court.

My assistant was a former football star from Oklahoma. He'd played linebacker at the University of Missouri and was once offered an audition by the New York Giants but decided to keep his brain intact and take a job as a biologist instead. His name was Doug.

One day in autumn the curatorial staff got a call from a Queens cop that two whales, a big one and a little one, had washed up on the beach at Far Rockaway. We jumped in Doug's car and went to investigate. The sky was leaking cold rain. We found the cop and his partner sitting warm and dry and sipping coffee in their squad car near the beach. They got out, and the four of us trooped down to the surf. I recognized the animals as a female pygmy sperm whale and her calf. The calf was a newborn, its umbilicus still attached. Taking the whales back to the aquarium with us was out of the question. The mother alone was nearly nine feet long and weighed several hundred pounds—not exactly appropriate cargo for the backseat of a Volkswagen Beetle.

A heavy truck with a tail-lift was inching toward us, its crew setting out a line of steel trash cans along the beach. We waved it down, flashed identification, and told the guys they needed to pick up the whales and follow us to Coney Island. They said they were just drivers and didn't have the authority. Doug and I told them we were authority enough, which we weren't, and to get their asses out of the truck and help us load the whales onto their lift. The truck had a radio, and the driver got his dispatcher to call our staff at the aquarium to be ready with stretchers and a forklift.

The whales went on display and were a sensation. Thousands of people came to see them. The aquarium's subway stop at Boardwalk and West 8th Street was packed. We extended public hours to accommodate everyone. The guy in charge of setting out the trashcans in Queens called my boss, the aquarium's director. He was furious that we'd commandeered his truck and crew. The director came into my office and handed me the guy's phone number and said, "You caused the problem. You deal with it."

I made the call saying, basically, that he was a hero for generously donating men and equipment to try and save these whales. I asked if he'd like to be on TV. Well, uh, sure, he said, and thanked me.

At the time Roger Grimsby, the six o'clock anchor on New York's WABC-TV, channel 7, was trudging down to the aquarium almost daily and reporting live on the condition of the whales. To a citizen of Manhattan, Coney Island might as well have been Siberia. Grimsby was grumpy and sarcastic off the air. Doug had an aw-shucks way of handling people that I never could match, and he got the trash-truck supervisor his interview.

The mother whale refused food and died. Her baby had never nursed and was too young to eat fish. We began using a stomach pump and feeding tube. Instead of pumping out the stomach, we reversed the positions of the hoses and pumped a warm blend of fish, evaporated milk, fish oil, and vitamins from a bucket into its stomach and set up a schedule for doing this every four hours. Either Doug or I was present for each feeding, assisted by another staff member.

We pulled on wet suits in the food preparation room, which was heated, then jumped into the shallow end of the outdoor pool where the baby whale was kept. The assistant held the whale with its head out of the water while Doug or I inserted the tube carefully down its throat and gently pumped in the requisite volume of formula. The whole process, including making the formula fresh each time, took about an hour. I covered the midnight feeding, Doug the feeding at four o'clock. Later ones occurred during normal work hours when we would both be there, one or the other taking over depending on who was less busy.

This continued for several weeks. I finally took my wetsuit home. Shortly before midnight I'd put it on in the apartment and walk down the boardwalk to the side entrance of the aquarium and let myself in with a passkey. The boardwalk at this time of night was poorly lit and unsafe. The second night I was approached by three young Hispanic men. It was too dark to see their faces. "Got a light?" one of them asked. It was his way of checking me out.

I made a show of unzipping the wetsuit and fumbling inside. "No," I said. "Too bad."

The guy said, "You're weird, man."

"It's Coney Island. Everybody's weird."

"Yeah, I know that, but they don't usually wear them frogman suits."

"Give them a chance," I said. "Anyway, I need mine to feed a baby whale."

This was enough to convince them I was not only unbalanced but likely dangerous. I watched as they traded glances, but I still couldn't see their eyes. They jabbered briefly among themselves in Puerto Rican Spanish. The dilemma was whether I was dangerously crazy and maybe had a weapon stashed in my "frogman suit," which came out literally *el traje del hombre rana.* They were obviously wary of a mugging attempt. The other two hadn't yet spoken to me directly; then one said, "Hey, cut the shit, man, you ain't feeding no fucking whale."

The third said, "Got any money, man?"

They were now asking for money instead of simply taking it. Still, I sensed a gain in confidence and decided to put them on the defensive again. "What the hell do you think? See any pockets?"

We waited in a standoff, no one moving. Finally I told them I had to go feed the whale and went on my way.

The next night, there they were again. The first to speak the previous night later told me his name was Julio. He seemed to be the leader. "Hey, man, I seen the whale on TV tonight, on the news. You know, Roger what's-his-face. You really the guy that feeds it?"

"One of them," I said. "We work as a team, sort of like y'all." Tonight the sky was clear, and I could see them grinning like sharks. Then I said, "Want to help me?"

We walked without speaking to the side gate, where I let us inside. Pedro was the curatorial staff member on duty to assist. He looked scared. "We have to talk," he whispered. I told Julio and his buddies to wait outside the door to the food preparation room and ducked inside with Pedro. "Those guys are muggers, and you let them in! Jesus, they'll kill us."

"I doubt it, "I said. "It's business as usual for us."

Pedro turned on the overhead lights, and we slid into the pool while the others stood along the edge. I tapped one of them on the leg, not Julio, but one of the others. "Hey you. Asshole. Hand me the bucket." They were awed by what was happening. "What the fuck's the matter, you deaf?" I said in a loud voice. He bent down and handed over the bucket. "Come to think of it," I said, "get down on your knees, hold the bucket steady, and lean over a little. That way I can pump out the formula. This is a baby whale. It's too young to eat fish like adult whales, so we feed it this baby whale formula through the tube I'm inserting into its stomach. Now hold the bucket steady because if the tube sucks air it'll make the whale sick. Got it?"

He nodded uncertainly. Pedro looked at me and rolled his eyes. Everything went smoothly. After a freshwater rinse under the outdoor shower I told the guys it was time to leave, and they followed me through the gate and waited while I locked up. Pedro left through the front gate to his car in the parking lot, no doubt glad to escape.

"That was so fucking cool!" Julio said. "Man, I can't fucking believe it. We fed a fucking whale!"

They waited for me outside the high-rise entrance every night and helped feed the whale, arguing about whose turn it was to hold the bucket. They stroked the whale, saying it felt like a wet inner tube, and they asked if whales ever became tame, whether you could teach them to talk like you could a parrot, and so forth. I told them that smoking around the whale was bad for it, and they believed me. One night as we were walking toward the gate I mentioned that a camera crew from channel 7 was coming over and asked if they'd like to be shown on TV helping out. They were ecstatic, until Julio abruptly dumped on the party atmosphere. "Aw shit, man," he said. "We're on parole and ain't supposed to be out this late. If our PO sees us on the news he'll know and bust us. Goddammit!"

I said I understood, but they could come back tomorrow night when it would be just me and an assistant.

The whale died shortly after this, unable to survive our crude attempt to devise an artificial whale milk. I'd based the composition on literature values for the milk of other whales, notably those killed commercially. The available information had been sparse and our result a poor facsimile.

There was a short blurb on the news. Figuring Julio might have missed seeing it, I stepped outside that night as if still in the routine, except I was wearing street clothes. They were waiting. I told them what had happened, explained why as best I could, and thanked them for helping. They cursed softly, looking down at their feet.

These guys had become personally involved with that baby whale, a creature so strange and wonderful as to render all previous experiences trivial. The event had been huge. All of New York had talked about it, and here they were, right in the middle. We'd come together in a random bump of Brownian motion, stuck for an instant, and then flung apart, leaving us all with memories similar to dreams. But there was something else. Maybe for the first time in their lives they'd pushed aside selfishness, fear, and uncertainty and invested a piece of themselves.

Julio lit a cigarette, his face flashing yellow in the glow off his cupped hands. He waved the match dead and tossed it aside. Handshakes all around.

"Well, fuck it, man," he said. "We better get to work, know what I mean? Got a quota to fill. See you around, maybe." His companions laughed, and they disappeared into the night.

# *Freddy*

Everything about Freddy was peculiar. He walked with short steps, feet splayed like the hands of a clock showing nine fifteen. It was the only thing that kept him from mincing. His stomach protruded well past where the toes of his shoes should have ended, and his arms and legs, seemingly stuck to the porky torso as an afterthought, were way too short. He had a quizzical smile, a permanently red face, and disturbing eyes magnified behind Coke-bottle glasses that left a feeling of having burrowed into your soul. All in all, he projected the look and demeanor of a deranged cherub. We never knew his last name. He told us only that it was Jewish and rhymed with "bagel."

Nothing is exactly as it seems, and sometimes even illusion itself is illusory. What Freddy showed to the world was merely one of many façades, none actually him. "What you see before you," he told us right after we met, "isn't really Freddy, but it's a reasonable facsimile. That should be good enough. If not, too bad because it's the best this Jewboy can do."

Then he'd sipped his gin and tonic and said something else in a self-deprecating way before circling around to the original subject and saying that what we were seeing—the fat piece of shit sitting between us looking at our collective selves in the mirror behind the bartender—wasn't the true him. As I said, this was when we first knew him, and we must have seemed puzzled, so he tried to clear matters by saying, "I can show you the true me, but that won't be him either."

"You're a big help, Freddy," Doug had said. "I feel much better after this talk."

The bar where we sat was inside a gym in Sheepshead Bay, Brooklyn. At our backs, lithe women in leotards astride machines like chromed horses pumped up and down in sweaty rhythm to some kind of crappy music busting out of the ceiling. Their reflections showed in the mirror before us, behind our own faces and the bartender's back. The place was hard-surfaced and loud. Echoes of speech and laughter collided incoherently, ricocheting off every sharp corner, every dumbbell and cocktail glass, dampened only by human flesh.

Most of the light came from TVs around the perimeter, each showing a different channel at full volume. People wearing swimsuits and shorts and tank tops were lounging on chaises. It could have been South Beach in Miami until you looked out a window and saw snowflakes tumbling past the streetlights.

Doug thought he should get back in football shape, tight and ripped the way he was in college, but not so much he'd need to quit cigarettes, so one day after work we hopped the subway at Boardwalk and West 8th Street station near the aquarium. Doug knew the address. While he pumped weights, I swam laps in the pool. Then we showered, dressed, and went to the bar. Freddy was there. As we learned later, he was usually there. He told us he lived with his mother within walking distance and never went anywhere else, socially, that is.

Mirrors are the sorcerer's ally, his tools of illusion, and this gym had them in spades. Everywhere you looked a human form bounced into view, some fractured where angled mirrors had been set. Depending on the location the pieced-together images were beautiful, ordinary, even grotesque. They could be dim or bright, quiescent or gyrating. The angles bent spines and stretched skulls, wedged lips open in twisted screams. It was a perfect stage for Freddy, although as I'll explain his performances were scattered elsewhere, away from here.

To understand Freddy's involvement in this maelstrom, start by finding a volunteer amputee experiencing phantom limb pain, say a guy who's lost his right arm. The effect is entirely mental, of course, because a limb that isn't there can't feel anything, including pain. Present him with one of Vilayanur Ramachandran's boxes containing two opposing mirrors. Have the guy put his left arm in one side of the box parallel to the left mirror and his stump in the other. The stump doesn't extend into the box, so what he sees on that side isn't a stump but a mirror image of the arm that's whole, the left one. Being the left arm's mirror image, it looks like a right arm. By unclenching his fist or bending his left elbow his stump becomes unkinked, and the pain goes away as if by magic.

Freddy's whole being was a missing limb in phantom pain, and what he stuck into this outsized mirror box on vacant evenings was himself. From a barstool he could spin around and look over the workout room and watch muscle-heads with perfect forms, teeth like vanilla ice cream, hair long and wavy as a thoroughbred's mane, and skin crisped to the color of a sunset by pretending to be a temporary corpse in one of those tanning coffins laid end to end outside the showers.

Why the interest? Freddy wasn't queer. He'd told us that himself, and we believed him. Those guys were what he saw reflected back from the mirror image of himself, the amputee's false reflection of his stump. He knew them all and bought them drinks. They stopped by regularly for a joke and a handshake, usually with a babe attached. One guy in particular, whose name was also Freddy, always asked when the next shoot was scheduled, what the wheels would be this time. Our Freddy would laugh, extend the little finger of his right hand and with the thumb pointed up, put the hand to his ear. "I'll call you youse," he'd say.

Finally it came out. We were bellied up to the bar earlier than usual. Doug had changed his mind about working out. It was summer, and I'd stopped doing laps in the pool because I was swimming home from work instead of walking, changing into a swimsuit at the office and leaving through the aquarium's boardwalk gate. Freddy had never asked us what we did for a living, and we'd never asked him either.

"So, what do youse do? For a living, I mean," Freddy said.

"We rescue penguins," Doug said.

"You mean from oil spills and such, washing the grease off them, right? Their feathers, right?"

"No," I said, "mostly we rescue them from bars in Coney Island where the knuckleheads usually take them."

"I don't get it," said Freddy.

Doug said, "We're from the New York Aquarium. Just today the 60th precinct called and said some drunks at a bar off Ocean Parkway had one of our penguins from the outdoor exhibit. They'd climbed over the fence along the boardwalk and stolen it as a joke or on a bet or something. Or possibly because they're stupid."

"So we went there," I said, "and there it was waddling around on top of the bar, slogging through spilled draft, and everyone laughing like hell. We boxed it up and took it back to the exhibit."

Freddy ordered a round. "That's too fucking weird," he said.

"Your turn," Doug said.

"Me?" said Freddy, acting surprised. "Not much, I'll tell you. I write for magazines."

He'd been content to leave matters there, but we kept prodding until he finally confessed.

"Okay, okay. Ever hear of these rags?" He listed a half-dozen popular motorcycle and car and driver 'zines common on every newsstand. They were top-shelf gearhead slicks. He was, he told us, a sort of test-driver journalist, a guy who powered up the latest product and put it through its paces out on the highways and along city streets—not race-tracks—where real people would be driving them. It was hard to picture Freddy even getting his feet straight enough to drive a car.

Afterward he'd write a detailed review explaining everything about the vehicle, good and bad. "You got to critique it all: the dashboard knobs and overhead lights, size of the glove box and trunk, handling on roads wet and dry, quality of the paint and finish, and all the moving parts. Is it quick off the mark? Do the gears shift like butter, is vision unobstructed all around? Leave out a detail and someone writes the editor and jumps on your shit. I do cars and bikes, but not trucks. I won't touch trucks. Nobody with any class drives a goddamn truck."

Months later, while killing time in a used bookstore near the boardwalk, I picked up a back issue of a magazine Freddy had mentioned. It was a couple of years old. Right there, the lead article, was a review of the new '70 Corvette under Freddy's byline. The brief author's bio in a side box said he lived in Manhattan and had been racing and evaluating high-performance cars and motorcycles for more than fifteen years. The photo showed a handsome greaser wearing a muscle shirt and jeans, an obvious bodybuilder with a gigolo's sincere white smile and a waist that might have matched the real Freddy's neck size. He looked familiar, but I couldn't be sure. According to the bio, Freddy had a degree in mechanical engineering and was a consultant to race drivers across the country.

It was lunchtime on a nice fall day. I bought a knish, found an empty bench, and started reading. The piece was written in that macho jargon you expect when entertainment intersects with man and machine and its author is a knowledgeable journalist, engineer, and connoisseur of internal combustion out to test the limits of an exquisite automobile.

> So, what's new with the 1970 Corvette? For the first time ever the base price of the most slimmed-down model tops five large, not exactly chump change unless you're a self-inflated Wall Streeter. The 4-speed manual tranny is now standard, meaning there is no 3-speed option, a step forward in this reviewer's opinion. Fender flares have been made an integral part of the body, which should go a long way toward eliminating damage from road debris.
>
> The model we tested was powered by a 427ci engine generating 435 galloping horses that would not quit. When idling, the little monster shivered and shook and gave out that inimitable 4-barrel rumble of 'vettes of all vintages, leaving no doubt about who's the meanest cat

> in the jungle. And does it hop? No, it leaps. Pop the clutch and feel all four paws leave the ground.
>
> When I revved at a standstill and tromped it, my co-pilot's stopwatch clicked in a lightning 6.8 seconds from 0–60 mph, just slightly slower than the official rating of 6.6. But consider this: our test drive took place on a blocked-off suburban street, not the groomed surface of a track. (Thank you, nice policemen. You've all earned a ride in my borrowed jet). In the quarter-mile, *Car Life* cranked the same model to 98.6 miles per in 14.6 seconds. Unfortunately, our law enforcement friends declined a request to test this statistic, citing permanent hearing loss in the neighborhood children if we pierced the sound barrier.

IT WENT ON, NOT EVERYTHING champagne and roses. Freddy hadn't liked the interior, a chronic GM design deficiency in his view, writing that he'd seen leather of better quality on a Kmart couch. The dash and control knobs were cheesy, and during its next school holiday the 'vette interior design team might want to make a field trip to the Porsche factory. There was more, of course. The article was several pages long. I kept wondering, could Freddy have written it?

I thought I'd check. Doug and I hadn't worked out in several weeks. It was winter again. One evening I hopped the D train to Sheepshead Bay, got off at the usual stop, and walked to the gym. On opening the door I was hit with the expected blast of warm humid air along with a strong odor of nitrogen trichloride, evidence of a badly managed swimming pool. So far, nothing had changed.

Freddy wasn't at the bar. I sat and ordered a drink. Just then the other Freddy, the fake one, came into view. I recognized him instantly and waved him over. He took a seat and told the bartender he'd have the usual.

He said, "I used to see youse and your friend hanging with Freddy. The fish guys, right? From the aquarium over in Coney Island."

"Right," I said. I told him my name, and we shook hands. I took out the magazine, which had been folded lengthwise and stuffed inside my coat pocket. "Here's your picture, Freddy, right beside Freddy's article about the '70 Corvette."

"My name ain't Freddy," he said. "My name's Danny." We shook again. He was looking at me and smiling, showing off his perfect teeth looking blue-white under the subterranean fluorescents.

"So does Freddy test these cars and bikes and write the articles? Is he an engineer?"

Danny's elbow stayed anchored on the bar. He tilted his head up and let his lower jaw protrude to lip his glass, giving an assist to gravity. "Freddy a fucking engineer? Now that's a good one."

I showed him Freddy's bio. He studied it and handed it back. "To tell the truth, I never bothered reading that before. Reading ain't my thing, exactly. I'll tell you this: except for cabs, the only wheels Freddy ever rode was the F train. He'd take it to Manhattan and see the suit who owns them magazines. Freddy himself never even got a driver's license. He took a cab here and left in a cab, always alone.

"Freddy was like one of them food critics who if he don't like the meal, what he writes can put the best restaurant in town in the dumper. The car and motorcycle dealers, they was scared shitless he'd give their product a bad review, know what I mean? They would've kissed his ass all the way down to the haunches, maybe even slipped him some green, only nobody knew him. What you seen in them pictures was me, not him, and they didn't know my name neither." Danny shook his head in admiration. "What a pisser, huh?"

"I read his review of the '70 'vette, the article I just showed you. It came out a couple of years ago. He made up that stuff?"

Danny laughed. "Freddy never even sniffed a 'vette

up close, guaranteed. Drive one? Are you outta your fucking mind?"

"So you got paid?"

"Naw, I done it for Freddy 'cause I like him. He's a great con man. And I done it a little for me. Plus it's fun. I show them stories with my picture around the gym for chuckles. Freddy's always buying drinks and saying nice things to the girls. Everyone thinks he's just a bullshitter, like the whole thing is a fucking joke. What a gas." He grinned.

"Broads was always writing to the editor wanting Freddy's phone number, meaning my phone number. The guy gives all the letters to Freddy when he comes over to Manhattan, and Freddy, he gives them to me. If the chick's local I call her, set up a meet, and maybe get laid. It's like one hand, how do you say it, helping the other, right?"

"Where's Freddy been lately?"

"Dunno. Ain't seen him in weeks. Anyhow, Freddy ain't his real name."

"What is it?"

Danny's leather jacket shrugged. "He never said, and I never ast him."

"He told me he lived with his mom here in Sheepshead Bay."

"Could be." He raised his empty glass my way. "'Nother hit?"

I envied Freddy. Like him, I'd always wanted to accomplish something while staying invisible. I looked in the mirror and coveted every woman I saw reflected there. I yearned to find the perfect one and disappear inside her darkest spaces, to float blindly in her amniotic fluid and emerge a child of sunshine and snow. I wondered then if Freddy had finally stepped into his own reflection or into another guy's somewhere else.

I'd been expected to stand out, to be somebody. That was always the message. Maybe the reflection and I had somehow changed places, and the reflection was real instead of the object. What then? My search for knowledge was just a deception, a distraction from the real point, which was invisibility.

A power failure brought the little world around to a hush, then everything was suddenly back as before. "Fuck," the bartender muttered. "Fucking ConEd bastids."

But in those seconds everything changed. I'd had an epiphany. Einstein's famous equation $E = mc^2$ works in both directions: matter can be converted to energy, but the reverse is also true, and the slowing of light waves causes them to attain mass. If matter is ethereal, so is objective reality, and if subatomic particles can sometimes be energy instead of matter then everything recognizable is simply static light; that is, light behaving as matter. The photons reflected onto my retina from the mirror had originally fled the stars. The objective "me" comprised atoms pushed apart by photons, making me a hologram not different from the Universe itself. My reflection and I were one. Whether Freddy or his reflection was the more real became irrelevant. We were all invisible.

I still see people sitting in bars not understanding how quickly the fragile moment passes, how existence is a blink of starlight lasting less than a cosmic second. They laugh and flirt and sometimes touch, unaware that the whispering wind against their lips contains no mention of eternity.

# *Hudson Bay*

BELUGA WHALES LIVE IN ARCTIC seas where waters are so cold that a human could survive about fifteen minutes, maybe less. Belugas are adapted to this harsh environment by being wrapped in a thick layer of blubber, which insulates them from the cold, and their circulatory systems have evolved to direct the flow of warm blood to areas of the body that are coldest and need heat the most.

The term "beluga" is also used to describe a fish inhabiting Russian waters. Its eggs are used to make the world's finest and most expensive caviar. To prevent confusing the beluga whale (a mammal) with the sturgeon (a fish), Russians call the whale "belukha." This has always been my preference because it keeps the distinction clear. In Canada belukhas are also called "white whales," and adults are indeed white. Baby belukhas, being born gray, gradually pale with age. Many years ago sailors in the Arctic called these whales “sea canaries” because they make high-pitched sounds similar to small songbirds.

In the early 1970s I took a job in Coney Island, which is a section of Brooklyn, New York. My position was curator of the New York Aquarium and Osborn Laboratories of Marine Sciences. These facilities are located directly on the famous boardwalk that follows along the beach, and in summer there are thousands of people sunbathing, swimming, and walking around eating ice cream and popcorn. Coney Island is also the place where Nathan’s hot dogs were first sold, and it has the country’s oldest roller coaster, the famous Cyclone, which was next door to the Aquarium’s executive offices and practically outside my window. I could hear the people shrieking and the roller coaster cars rushing past. The noise was distracting at first, but slipped eventually into the background and I stopped noticing it.

The New York Aquarium had several belukhas back then, and during my stay the first birth ever of a captive specimen occurred in one of our exhibits. The baby lived only eight minutes, banging into a wall and then drowning before we could save it. Still, this was a remarkable event, and as the person responsible for the care of all the animals I set out to learn everything I could about the species.

The whales were already in residence when I took the job, having been captured years before by my predecessor, Carleton Ray. Dr. Ray had left the organization for a professorship at the University of Virginia, but I had known him from conferences where marine scientists gather to share knowledge. After the birth of the baby belukha I contacted Carleton, and he sent me a package of his notes from trips to the Arctic during which he studied belukhas in the wild and explained how he had managed to capture them for the aquarium.

Before a federal law called the Marine Mammal Protection Act was passed in 1972, it was legal to capture any species of marine mammal whether a whale, dolphin, seal, sea lion, or walrus simply by setting forth and doing it. But the new ruling changed that. Permits from the federal government were now necessary, and these became difficult to procure because many people believed it was inhumane to keep marine mammals in captivity. In their view, the public display of live animals ought to be made illegal. Their attempts in this direction failed, so they took the position of making the acquisition of live specimens extremely difficult by protesting the issuance of capture permits.

The Coney Island whales had been captured long before this law took effect. One of ours, a big male named Alex, had been caught by Dr. Ray and his team in Bristol Bay, Alaska, in 1961 shortly after his birth and flown by chartered aircraft to New York. The seawater in our pools was pumped continuously from deep beneath the sands of Coney Island beach, and it registered a near-constant 52°F all year, cold enough to be comfortable for creatures indigenous to northern seas.

The other whales had been captured in Canada. When I talked to Carleton, he explained why. In those years there was an aboriginal fishery for belukhas. The local Inuits (also known as Eskimos) harpooned them at the mouth of the Churchill River, which flows east for a thousand miles through Alberta, Saskatchewan, and Manitoba before emptying into the Hudson Bay. A whaling station at the village of Churchill, Manitoba, then stripped off the blubber and boiled it to make whale oil, which was sold as a food additive. The meat was ground into pet food or sold to mink and fox farms. In other words, Carleton said, there were already experienced Inuits eager for work who would gladly catch whales alive instead of killing them. They used large (eighteen-foot) wooden canoes powered by outboard motors to chase down the whales and herd them into shallow areas of the river. For live-capture, Carleton and one of the local whalers, a hulking man with a bodybuilder's frame named John Hickes, whose mother was Inuit and whose father was a French Canadian trapper, devised a method of picking out a suitable whale and jumping on its back.

The technique worked like this. One end of a stout rope was tied to the bow of a canoe, the other fashioned into a loop, like a lasso. The idea was to maneuver the canoe parallel with a fleeing whale. A man standing in the bow wearing a wetsuit and holding the loop then dived headfirst at the whale, hoping to slip the noose over its head. Belukhas lack a dorsal fin, so the loop was expected to slide down the length of the body and cinch tightly when it hit the base of the tail, tethering the animal to the canoe, literally catching it by its tail.

Once a whale had been secured by the rope, others in the capture crew jumped overboard and slid the thrashing animal into a thick canvas stretcher, the poles of which were attached to the side of the canoe in a sort of outrigger arrangement. It was obviously best if the whale could be chased into shallow water so its captors could stand on the river bottom and thus gain leverage.

Because the stretchers weren't lifted out of the water, the canoe didn't become unbalanced unless the whale struggled excessively, although capsizing was not uncommon. The boatman then drove slowly back to shore. The whale's movements could be further restricted by bringing the far pole of the stretcher close to the first and strapping it to the side of the canoe. The poles were heavy steel, able to support the weight of a whale weighing nearly half a ton. Once the canoe reached shore as many men as could be assembled lifted the animal in its stretcher and carried it across the mudflats to a portable swimming pool. The task was more difficult at low tide (the Churchill is a tidal river), when every step meant sinking into sometimes knee-deep mud.

Jumping on the back of a fleeing whale was always exciting and often dangerous, as my first jump illustrates. Our several canoes were meandering around in the river mouth when a pod of whales came puffing in from Hudson Bay. Someone yelled, and we gave chase, canoes zooming around with everyone hanging on tightly so as not to be tossed overboard. We were all wearing thick wetsuits, but the water was very cold, and there was no point in getting dunked unnecessarily.

The boat I was in came alongside a snow-white whale. It was swimming at full speed and seemed unusually big to me. Adults can weigh up to 3,200 pounds, and the specimens we were targeting were between seven hundred and a thousand pounds—adolescents, in other words, and they would be pale gray. Ordinarily only full-grown adult belukhas are white. I was crouched in the bow holding a lasso, the canoe lurching forward over the low waves when someone behind me yelled, "Jump him!"

In the excitement I stood up and dived headfirst onto the whale, slipping the noose over its head and then hanging on as best I could. The whale sensed the rope tighten against the base of its tail and went berserk, thrashing and rolling violently. I was dragged underwater, the force of the explosion pushing my face into the mud of the riverbed. The moment was reminiscent of falling off a surfboard and feeling the wave I'd just missed drive me to the sea floor. My chest and right side shot through with pain as if I'd been stabbed.

I surfaced to see laughing faces hanging over the gunwale and hands stretched out to help me aboard. The whale was gone. "What the hell?" I said.

One of my boat mates said, "Sorry, but it's our initiation for new jumpers. We never jump whales when they're white. That was a full-size bull. We cut him loose right after he bucked you off."

"Thanks lots," I said, holding my side. Every breath was painful. The veterinarians later taped my chest, and X-rays after we got home revealed a cracked rib and torn cartilage around the sternum. The injuries didn't stop me from jumping more whales over the next several days, but as a result of that experience I looked closely at the quarry, taking note of its color and estimating its size before leaping on its back.

After I left Coney Island to help build a new public aquarium in Mystic, Connecticut, I was replaced by Bill, an old friend and Brooklyn native who had worked there previously in a lesser capacity. This time he returned home as curator, having resigned a similar position at SeaWorld, San Diego. Real New Yorkers, the joke goes, can't trust air they can't see, and Bill was grateful to leave sunny southern California for the gray east coast. I was grateful, too, because Bill had been Carleton's chief assistant on two Canadian expeditions to catch belukhas. He knew how to get things done, and willingly pooled his organization's resources with ours in financing a joint expedition to bring back whales for both aquariums. The joint venture then became a matter of obtaining permits and plotting the logistics.

Bill and I negotiated. I told him I wanted Alex, who was getting old, in trade for a young male belukha now swimming around somewhere in western Hudson Bay. Mystic Aquarium would pay for this as yet uncaught whale and fly it to JFK International Airport, at which point Bill would be responsible for its transport to Coney Island. Mystic, in turn, would pay to truck Alex up I-95 to our facility. New York would pay for Bill and his staff to accompany my crew to Churchill. We planned on catching four whales, two for each facility. The first one caught would be Bill's. If he rejected that one Mystic could keep it or release it and we'd continue hunting. That was the plan, catch and release until we had four healthy whales and both institutions were satisfied. Coming along as an observer would be Dr. Wolfgang Gewalt, director of Duisburg Zoo in what was then West Germany. Dr. Gewalt was planning a new whale exhibit and wanted to learn how to capture belukhas, care for them in the field, and ship them by air. His institution was paying his expenses.

Soon after the US passed the Marine Mammal Protection Act of 1972, Canada passed a similar bill. We therefore needed US permits to import belukhas and keep them in captivity, plus capture and export permits from Canada's federal agency, Environment Canada, and still others from the provincial government of Manitoba where the capture would take place. All applications would necessitate public hearings where citizens and organizations opposed to our applications could speak against us or submit written comments. There was a comment period and afterward evaluation by governmental regulatory agencies.

Securing the necessary documents took more than a year. Meanwhile we made extensive lists of all equipment needed for the fieldwork. Once on site we had to be self-contained. There were no spare parts or substitutes available if, say, a motor or pump malfunctioned. In fact, Churchill might not have existed at all were it not a seaport and ice-free during a few weeks of mid-summer. Grain from Canada's vast prairie provinces arrives from the west by rail to be warehoused at a huge storage facility just outside the village. Ships from Europe and Asia arrive to load it and depart before ice starts forming again in September.

Curatorial personnel in Mystic and New York made lists and checked them for duplicates, eliminating items where necessary and adding others. Everything for capturing whales, holding them temporarily onshore in portable swimming pools erected on site, and shipping them back would be sent ahead by rail to Churchill. The railroad from Winnipeg, Manitoba's largest city, to Churchill crosses a thousand miles of tundra, a thin marsh in summer and a frozen wasteland in winter. Our consignment would be examined by Canadian customs agents at Winnipeg, shipped on to Churchill, and stored there inside a government warehouse.

Maintenance personnel in Mystic built two sturdy, watertight boxes of wood and lined them with foam rubber and polyethylene sheeting. New York's staff built two on the same plan. Each box was designed to hold a whale up to nine feet long and weighing perhaps eight hundred pounds. The stretcher poles fit into notches at the ends of the boxes, suspending the whales a few inches above the bottom. Water collected in a sump underneath the animals was returned by submersible pumps to devices that sprayed them continuously to keep their skins moist, and the hundreds of pounds of ice we would load onto the plane before departure would be sprinkled along the inside edges of the stretchers to prevent overheating. A whale encased in blubber tends to become too hot when removed from the water. The plane, a Boeing 737 chartered from Air Canada, had seats for the flight crew and our two staffs. All other seats would be removed beforehand to make room for whales and equipment.

Included in the equipment shipped ahead was a portable microbiology laboratory. Starting with the 1984 expedition I took along Patricia, my laboratory technician, who would collect bacteriological samples from Churchill River and Hudson Bay waters, and from the whales themselves, and begin culturing them using space and facilities donated by the small medical clinic in Churchill. Swabs were taken from the blowhole, anus, and surface skin of every whale caught to assess its normal microbiota. Back home, the cultures would be turned over to Dr. John Buck, a colleague at the University of Connecticut Department of Marine Sciences for subculture and identification. Subsequent samples would allow us to compare the normal microbiology of belukhas in the wild with changes induced by captivity. Veterinarians Emil Dolensek representing the New York Aquarium and Larry Dunn from Mystic would draw blood samples from the newly-captured whales and make a preliminary assessment of their general health. Additional samples would be frozen under Pat's direction for more detailed analysis in the United States.

These Canadian expeditions were bureaucratic nightmares of paperwork and scheduling, arranging for contacts in the field, and the seemingly endless details required in the logistics of any big, mobile project. But it was also lots of fun. I made three such trips in total, the first in July 1975 and two more in August 1984 and 1985. Much of what I discovered could only have been learned on the job. For example, John Hickes had warned me not to get too friendly with his fellow Inuits and agree to hire them, emphasizing that I would be wise to leave that up to him. Did I listen? Not that first trip.

Churchill had two pubs separated by an alley not more than eight feet wide. At that time, Canadian law required bars to be closed several hours out of every twenty-four, the idea being that patrons might stay home some of the time, at least long enough to become reacquainted with their wives and children. Churchill's citizens had circumvented this inconvenient dilemma in a novel way. During my first trip I went to the bar soon after arriving in town, noticing vaguely the presence of a similar but darkened establishment across the alley.

My staff and I made ourselves comfortable, and I started buying beers for the locals and learning their names. Time passed, and the barman shouted last call. In my previous experience this would have caused a loud clamor for final rounds, but here no one paid attention. Then the lights flashed, indicating that closing was imminent. The barman took the cash drawer out of the register and set it on top of the jukebox. He unplugged the jukebox in the middle of a record, and the song, a country number, wound to a stop. He put the jukebox with the cash drawer on a hand truck and wheeled it across the alley, where he opened the other bar and switched on the lights. He plugged in the jukebox, and the same song came to life. He slipped the cash drawer into an identical register.

The patrons, carrying their drinks, followed him. The new bar was a mirror image of the other. We sat in replicas of the same chairs in the same part of the room as before. When I eventually tottered back to the Beluga Motel, at least a half-dozen Inuits came too, and they spent the rest of the night sleeping on the floor outside my room. Some didn't sober up right away, which delayed the whale hunt and put us a day behind schedule.

The mouth of the Churchill River is a historical gathering site where polar bears wait for the ice on the Hudson Bay to form and thicken, after which they spend the winter far out on the ice hunting seals. In summer they live ashore with nothing to eat. A starving bear is a grumpy bear, and wandering around on the tundra can be dangerous. Although the land is flat and marshy, it's amazingly easy for a bear to lie among the dwarf willows and other vegetation and remain invisible.

In those days the village dumped its garbage outside town, and bears foraged there regularly. Occasionally a bolder one came into town and broke into people's houses. At such times wardens from Environment Canada, working with Canadian Mounties, would dart the offending animal using an anesthetic and haul it to the "bear jail," a place of sturdy steel cages near the town dump. Multiple offenders were airlifted by helicopter far out on the tundra away from town and released. Still, there were incidents, and once a local drunk passed out on the street and a wandering bear chewed off his arm.

Belukhas were very popular exhibit animals, and when the Minnesota Zoo opened in Apple Valley, Minnesota, one of the main attractions was to be a whale exhibit. I had assisted the zoo with designing its new facility, and the director called one day. He said he'd heard that New York and Mystic were planning a joint expedition to Churchill and asked if his young veterinarian could come along to gain some experience with whales. His expenses would be paid by the zoo, and he would serve as assistant to our vets. Bill and I agreed.

Minnesota Zoo's vet met us at JFK, where we all took a commercial flight to Winnipeg. I forget his name, but he was a personable guy just out of veterinary college. He seemed eager to learn all he could. On arrival at the motel in Winnipeg we adjourned to a tavern across the street. Our new friend soon spied an attractive Inuit girl across the room and lost interest in animal medicine. She was from Churchill and would be on the flight with us the next morning. That night they shared his room, and when we arrived in Churchill he cancelled his room at the Beluga Motel and took up cohabitation with his new friend.

This was not inconvenient because he showed up each morning ready to work. When the expedition was over, he was to fly back to Minnesota commercially, not on our chartered plane. There was one flight a week round trip between Winnipeg and

Churchill. Gathering at the airfield was a social event. Many Churchill residents had relatives or friends in Winnipeg, plus it was the only chance the local dealers had to make a regular dope run. Not surprisingly, the whole village was usually on hand to see the plane land and depart.

When our work ended the whole capture team showed up to see our new associate off and wish him well. Everyone was standing near the plane waiting to board or wave goodbye to someone else who was boarding. Suddenly a group of Hickes' brothers and other Inuit men broke through the crowd and grabbed our young friend. They wrestled him to the ground, pulled off his boots and pants, jerked him to his feet, and left him standing in his underwear. "Let this be a lesson to all you dirty white men who come up here just to screw nice Eskimo girls!" they yelled. "Yeah, that'll teach you!" shouted the crowd. Their laughter was deafening. Then John Hickes grinned and handed the guy his pants and boots, and as he climbed red-faced up the gangway still in his skivvies the whole village and everyone seated on the plane gave him a round of applause.

Mrs. Hickes, John's mother, was Inuit, and she had two husbands, one Inuit and the other (John's father) French Canadian. According to what I was told by George Hickes, one of John's younger brothers, the arrangement came about in this way. The original husband was Inuit. He worked trap lines in winter with his dog team and sold the skins of animals he trapped—mostly Arctic foxes and Arctic hares. One day he came across an injured fellow trapper, a French Canadian, who would surely have frozen to death. The Inuit took him home, saving his life. According to custom, when you save someone's life you become responsible for that person, which, in this case, evidently included sharing your wife.

Mrs. Hickes had twelve children, eleven boys and a girl. She knew the father immediately by each baby's color. All the children were close in age, separated by only a year or two, and the boys formed an amateur hockey team called simply the Hickes brothers, and for several years were league champions throughout the Canadian northwest from Winnipeg to Yellowknife and beyond. The daughter became a flight attendant for Air Canada and frequently worked the round trip between Winnipeg and Churchill. She was half French Canadian, attractive, and soon after we became acquainted she complained bitterly that having eleven brothers all determined to protect her maidenhood had become a detriment to her ever finding a boyfriend, much less a husband.

The village threw a party at the community center to celebrate success after the 1985 expedition. There was lots of beer and dancing to a record player, but the only song seemed to be "Woolly Bully" by Sam the Sham and the Pharaohs. It played at full volume over and over late into the bright night until everyone was loaded. Mrs. Hickes kept asking me to dance. She was well into her seventies and toothless, but she danced by grinding up against me and bumping pelvises, and when I eventually declined to participate she dragged me onto the floor and ordered, "Boy, you dance." Meanwhile John and George stood on the sidelines unable to stop laughing. I finally escaped and joined them.

It was inevitable, now that I think back. One of the guys produced a glass gallon jar packed with several gray gelatinous objects soaking in a cloudy liquid. Muktuk, someone said. Whale blubber sliced into chunks with the skin still attached. You need the skin, George explained, because that's where the vitamins are. And the liquid? Concentrated brine. There was no telling how old the stuff was, because commercial whale hunts had ended several years earlier, although local Inuits were permitted to kill a few whales annually in a "subsistence hunt" so they could freeze enough whale meat and blubber to feed their sled dogs through the winter.

The Inuit whalers gathered around urging me to try it. The stuff is delicious, they said. You'll like it, guaranteed. The jar lid was quickly unscrewed. I dipped my fingers inside and pulled out a chunk of muktuk about three inches square and popped it in my mouth while everyone watched intently. Nothing could have tasted more foul. After a minor swallow during which I nearly puked, I gagged up what was left and began spitting furiously, trying to get rid of the taste. Everyone started to laugh.

"How can you eat this shit?" I sputtered.

"We don't," said Sled Dog Mike. "Only stupid white people eat it. We eat potato chips."

THROUGHOUT CANADA, CITIZENS OF NEWFOUNDLAND (referred to as Newfies) are the objects of jokes and good-natured derision because of a supposed form of indigenous, provincial stupidity and sloth. Most are similar—even identical—to Irish and redneck jokes told in the States. A typical Newfie joke I heard from the Inuits asks: Why is a Newfie buried with his head and feet pointed down and his butt-crack above ground? The answer: Bicycle rack.

There was a Newfoundlander among our group of whalers, and his nickname, of course, was Newfie. He was slight and sandy-haired with a cigarette always stuck in his face. He never said much, and once I mentioned to George in an offhand way, "Newfie's so quiet you wonder what he's thinking."

"He can't think," George said. "He's a Newfie."

Newfie was legendary among the locals. He trapped in winter, and an Inuit helping work his trap lines once reported seeing Newfie shoot and then eat a ptarmigan, a sort of tundra quail. The thing was, Newfie ate it raw and left nothing behind. After picking out the lead shot (or most of it), he ate the head, beak, feathers, feet, guts, bones—everything. Then he belched, took a swallow of Canadian Club, and said, "Now that was mighty tasty."

# *Iced Up*

It was March 1983. I was director of Mystic Aquarium in Mystic, Connecticut. My office had a single window shaped like a porthole. I was standing in front of it looking out at the typical crappy weather, a mix of rain and snow, when Larry, our veterinarian, came through the door. He said a commercial fisherman had telephoned from his home in Fair Haven, Newfoundland, and reported a group of dolphins trapped in the ice inside a small bay nearby. He asked if we wanted to come get them and pay him to help us.

Times were tough for commercial fishermen from New England up through the Canadian Maritimes. Recent US and Canadian regulations had placed severe catch restrictions on cod, pollock, and other centuries-old staples of the trade, and many families who had fished for generations were being forced to stay ashore and find other work. Here was some easy money for the workingmen of this village of about two hundred residents, if we were willing to go. There were no legal issues at our end. We had permits to capture and display several species of dolphins and porpoises indigenous to the North Atlantic. The caller was unsure which these were, although they all seemed to be the same. We needed to act quickly.

Larry telephoned him back and said to give us a couple of days, that we had to organize equipment and charter a plane, get flight clearances, notify government authorities in both countries, and so forth. Our contact said the ice was drifting out, and he and a couple of associates would ring the dolphins inside a big net to hold them.

We called around to the local air charter services and found an available aircraft, a Conair 240 based at Quonset Point, Rhode Island, an hour or so away, and booked it round trip to St. John. From there we'd get a rental truck, load the transport equipment—including six big watertight boxes fitted with slings to hold the dolphins—and drive to Fair Haven on Placentia Bay, a distance of about eighty miles. Anyway, that was the plan. But lives are dynamic and easily disrupted by quantum events of unpredictable and sometimes frightening proportion. Serendipity, which had trapped those dolphins in an unnamed cove, was about to touch us too, and here I jump ahead in the narrative.

Rugged weather forced us out of the flight plan to St. John and an unexpected landing at Gander. After showing passports and cementing the next day's flight plan for continuing to St. John, we hopped a taxi to a nearby motel. The bar was overflowing with drunken Texas oil workers on the way home from an extended stay on a rig somewhere in the Canadian Arctic. Larry, Curt, and I joined them in a celebration of life. The pilots would be on duty in a few hours and reluctantly went to bed.

The next morning we telephoned our contact in Fair Haven. His wife answered and said her husband was looking after the dolphins. We told her we were in Gander delayed by weather, but would be taking off soon for St. John.

At St. John we loaded our equipment into the rental truck and headed for Fair Haven. The pilots would get a room at a nearby motel and wait for us to contact them through a number at the hangar. We hoped to reach Fair Haven that afternoon, look over the situation, devise a plan for extricating and loading the dolphins into the truck, and execute the procedure the following day. Assuming everything went well, we could take off shortly afterward and be back in Rhode Island by dawn.

The drive to Fair Haven took about three hours. We met our contact at his house and went to see the dolphins and start figuring out how to get them from the freezing ocean into our truck. We were planning to take back six animals, which meant catching all of them inside the net, examining each for approximate age, sex, and general health, wrestling those we wanted into stretchers, and lifting them into the transport boxes.

The animals turned out to be white-beaked dolphins, a species we hadn't encountered before. No one knew much about white-beaks, and to our knowledge they had never been kept in captivity. They were beautiful creatures, gray streaked with white along their upper sides and with white snouts and throats. They were also big (the smallest at least two hundred pounds) and lively, and separating the ones we wanted, subduing them, horsing them into stretchers, and lifting them out of the water wouldn't be easy. Luckily there were lots of unemployed fishermen standing around offering to help for a day's pay.

We decided not to wait until the next day. We stripped down and put on our thick wetsuits. Although most of the ice had left this section of the bay, the water was bitterly cold. Meanwhile the fishermen got into their boats, an assortment of aluminum rowboats and double-ended wooden dories, and started shipping in the net, making the circle's circumference ever smaller and forcing the dolphins toward land near where the truck was parked. The slings were taken out of the truck and lined up along the rocky shore, each supported in its frame of stout iron pipes. The three of us in the water got inside the net and started checking out the animals. There were perhaps a dozen, but with all the movement and splashing it was hard to tell.

We started selecting medium-sized individuals, holding them individually, trying to quiet them, and giving each a quick examination: skin and eye condition, condition of the fins and flippers, and turning them sideways to sex them. No specimen was clearly geriatric or newborn, and no female was lactating. All appeared to be adolescents or adults. We selected six we thought were adolescents, although we couldn't know for certain. After loading them into slings, the boatmen opened the two ends of the net and released the others, which made a hasty dash toward the open expanse of Placentia Bay. We made sure the animals were loaded safely, phoned the airport, and drove to St. John. The trip home was uneventful, a welcome change.

But back to the start of this story. A couple of days after receiving the call in Connecticut, Larry and I, along with Curt, who was in charge of the Aquarium's marine mammal training program, climbed aboard the plane at Quonset Point. Our equipment was tied down snugly with cargo nets. We buckled into jump seats while the pilot and co-pilot fired the engines. The plane sputtered and shuddered, then coughed like a sick old hound suddenly kicked awake. After revving for a time on the runway we lifted off with the grace of a crippled goose.

Insulation was minimal, perhaps nonexistent, and the cargo space soon felt like the inside of a meat locker. Engine noise, in concert with the loud rattling and shaking of the plane itself, made it necessary to shout at each other to be heard.

Although we were wearing goose-down jackets and gloves, jeans, watch caps, and hiking boots with thick socks, the cold eventually became unbearable, and we each picked out an empty transport box and climbed inside. The boxes, which were about eight feet long, had been lined with foam and covered in plastic to help retain melt-water from the ice that would later be sprinkled over the dolphins to keep them from overheating during conveyance.

Larry was working toward a pilot's license and wanted to log some flight time, so he and the co-pilot temporarily switched places. Night came on, and the interior illumination attenuated to a steady glow from the instrument panels in the cockpit and monotonous blinking of the navigation lights through the windows slashed increasingly with snow and sleet.

"Weather!" the pilot shouted over his shoulder. "We're coming into some weather, so hang on!"

The aircraft banged along like a crumbling truck on a washboard road. It dived and surfaced, twisted and groaned, occasionally tossing us into the air and slamming us back down. The co-pilot climbed out of his box and staggered to the cockpit to replace Larry. With worsening weather the plane seemed to stagger too, its plunges becoming deeper and more prolonged, each recovery and lift slower than the last. Noise from the laboring engines rose to an ear-splitting shriek. The windows had now become thick with ice. I got out of my box and stood and remembered a line from James Cameron's memoir *Point of Departure* in which he wrote that "the theory of aerodynamics is reasonable, but there is still no explanation of how the wings stay on." The riveted plates seemed to wobble and slide underfoot like the wooden planks of an old boat, imparting a rolling sensation of being at sea in a gale. I was almost expecting a cold wave to wash over us.

The co-pilot motioned me forward. He said we were icing up badly and would never last to St. John. Our only chance was Gander, and we were headed there instead. He said if we happened to be religious now would be a good time to start praying.

I reported back to Larry and Curt. I shouted that this could be it, the big casino, and mentioned our co-pilot's recommendation to pray. In one of the transport boxes containing wetsuits, dive gear, and knapsacks with spare clothes was a case of beer. Drinking beer at this moment of crisis seemed imminently more sensible than praying. You can never know when God might be paying attention, but one thing was certain: the beer would be cold.

We barely made Gander, dropping out of the black sky like a shot mallard before striking the ground heavily and lurching to a stop. Fire trucks stood by prepared to dispense water and fire-suppressant foam; police cars and ambulances idled beside them. Flashing lights streaked the wet runway and tinted the snow banks alternately red and blue. Sirens were going off, but they sounded distant and tame compared with the noise we'd just experienced. Our ears rang for days afterward.

The pilot muttered how he maybe shit his pants, but couldn't be sure. We five grabbed knapsacks, pushed the door open, and descended like royalty. Some posit how the living can never truly understand death. Count me among them.

# *Seal Stew*

I NEVER MET THE ENGLISH navigator Henry Hudson because he died in 1611, although I've shaken hands several times with his eponymous inland sea.

Hudson Bay has the shape of a cow's udder, and James Bay, the tit hanging off the bottom, represents the southern extent of the Arctic Ocean. Late in 1610, Hudson's vessel *Discovery* had sailed into this cul-de-sac. With the onset of winter it became stuck in the sea ice. Now marooned, the crew became increasingly hungry, cold, and pissed off at their captain. The following June, after the ice melted sufficiently, *Discovery* sailed north out of James Bay. The crew mutinied soon after, and at an unrecorded location Henry, his son John, and a few others were forced into a small boat and set drifting into the unknown. They probably died of exposure, but no one is really certain. All we know is they were not seen again.

In August 1985 I got to Churchill, a village on Hudson Bay's western shore, a week before the whale hunt to be certain all gear had arrived safely and was in working order. I was there to capture belukha whales for the public aquarium I worked for in Mystic, Connecticut.

We'd shipped a mountain of equipment by rail, and it was being stored in a government warehouse. After finding someone with a key and inspecting everything, I checked into the Beluga Motel, a rickety wooden structure near the mouth of the Churchill River where it empties into Hudson Bay. The inspection took a couple of hours, then I walked into the village for a beer. At the pub I ran into George Hickes. He was drinking with Sled Dog Mike and Newfie, two other locals I knew. George mentioned that he and his older brother and his brother's wife were leaving the next morning for the Seal River to shoot seals for their skins and he invited me to come along. The Seal River flows east into Hudson Bay parallel to the Churchill River about forty miles north. We would be taking one of the big canoes we used to catch whales. The plan was to camp a day or two at the river mouth and do the shooting at sea from the canoe.

We left the next morning headed north, following the coastline. George's older brother, whose name I forget, was pure Inuit, and his wife was also Inuit.

George, who was half French Canadian, was friendly and garrulous, but these two rarely spoke and never seemed to smile. When they conversed it was in Inuktitut, not a word of which I understood.

The time was early August, but the weather was cold. Ice in the Churchill River had just broken up, and large chunks were drifting past the Beluga Motel into the bay. Wind blowing onshore made conditions even colder because of the water temperature: when I dropped a thermometer on a string over the side, it registered 29°F, enough to add its own layer of damp chill. Conditions at the Seal River would be the same.

The sky was the color of a corpse, the weakened sun inked on it like a bad tattoo. I'd brought a sleeping bag and was wearing a watch cap, jeans, a goose-down jacket, hiking boots over two pairs of wool socks, leather gloves, and a thick wool shirt with a T-shirt underneath. George had brought along a few supplies: a bag of ground coffee, bacon and eggs, a cloth sack of dried pinto beans, a greasy paper bag filled with homemade jerked caribou from an animal shot the previous winter, and several quart bottles of Canadian Club.

The trip took about six hours. Just south of the river mouth we scrunched the boat onto a gravel beach where the stones seemed frantic in their loneliness. I tossed the bow anchor among them. A cold northeast wind was whipping up and turning the whitecaps toward our faces. Seaward, mist and distant squalls occluded the horizon. The last couple of hours had driven sea spray over us. Our clothes were soaked and I was starting to shiver, but my companions seemed oblivious to the chill. To our backs the tundra stretched flat and mostly featureless, interrupted here and there by quartzite ledges and dwarf willows squatting low against the wind.

George's sister-in-law had contributed a dented aluminum pot holding about a gallon, a similar pot of lesser size, a square metal pan, a plastic bucket, a cast-iron frying pan, some battered aluminum cups, a few spoons, and a galvanized washtub. She took the bucket and walked west along the bank a hundred yards or so upriver where she filled it with muddy water. The tide was out, and the surface water would be mostly fresh. The shoreline was littered with bleached driftwood looking like the ancient bones of extinct whales. We collected enough in a half-hour to burn through the night, a precaution against wandering polar bears, although only the loud report of a rifle was likely to deter a hungry bear homing in on the odor of our food.

Once a fire was going the sister-in-law put a pinch of snuff between her gum and lower lip and began boiling river water in the bigger pot. George and his brother lit cigarettes, I stuck a large chaw of Mail Pouch in my cheek, and we passed around the whisky. Supper was pinto beans boiled with jerked caribou, which gave it a gamey aftertaste that clung tightly to the tongue. We leaned forward almost touching heads and scooped it communally from the pot using the battered spoons. The wind died suddenly, and mosquitoes rose off the land in clouds, their whine almost deafening. Eventually we excavated shallow graves among the stones, unrolled our wet sleeping bags, and crawled inside under perpetual twilight. In the Arctic's brief summer the sun never sets completely, and stays bright enough to read a book even at midnight.

The next morning the sister-in-law scrambled bacon and eggs together in the frying pan. She filled the small pot with river water and made cowboy coffee by tossing a handful of coarse grind into boiling water for several minutes. Then George and his brother and I launched the boat and went to sea. The sister-in-law stayed on the beach to collect driftwood and keep the fire burning. Her husband left her a rifle in case a bear showed up. Before breakfast she had chewed his sealskin mukluks, stiff with the previous day's salt stains, to softness using her worn teeth and saliva, an old Inuit custom I hadn't seen enacted until then.

We motored a mile or so offshore and cut the engine. The water was clear and calm. A seal popped its head above the surface, and George killed it with a single shot from his lever-action .30-30. George's brother started the outboard and we raced to the spot, but the carcass sank before we got to it. That turned out to be the biggest problem. Seals were plentiful, but after being shot they disappeared quickly into the depths. We eventually retrieved one, an immature ringed seal weighing about forty pounds.

It started to rain. George squinted at the sky. "On a day like this, my people say the clouds are crying."

I told him that sounded like bullshit. "Do they really say that?"

"No, I made it up."

We'd drifted toward shore into a shallow zone where the sea's surface looked tranquil, but I knew that wasn't the case. The sea is never tranquil. Under the surface it writhes, simultaneously imbibing and expelling itself. The kelp on the floor of this sea was dancing in cruel syncopation to a silent dirge. It swung back and forth like a Gorgon's green hair.

Back ashore, George's brother skinned the carcass and stretched the skin on the beach, anchoring it with stones to hold its shape. When he slit open the naked carcass, steaming intestines spilled out and slithered over the wet stones as if trying to escape. His wife gathered them up, then dug around for the liver, kidneys, and heart, after which her husband sliced what remained in two pieces, one consisting of the head and front flippers, the other of the posterior half and hind flippers. The woman put the heart and liver in the little square pan for an appetizer we would eat raw. Then she washed the two halves of the seal, the kidneys, and the intestines in seawater, and put them in the washtub, which she filled with cold seawater and started simmering on the fire while she went off to collect more driftwood.

George sat down and twisted open a new bottle of Canadian Club. "Steve," he said, "do you know how an Eskimo cooks seal kidneys?"

"No," I answered.

"He boils the piss out of them," said George. His brother grinned at me. He had no teeth. He wiped his knife on a pants leg to clean off the seal blood and accepted the bottle passed his way. It was the only time I saw him smile.

We stayed at the Seal River three days, never completely drying out. Our time was spent shooting ringed seals, skinning them, and eating seal meat mostly rendered to unidentifiable pieces after having been boiled in seawater. It took fierce concentration to try and forget my knowledge of seal anatomy and pretend what I saw floating before me was simply a previously unrecognized form of seagoing hamburger. The efforts were mostly futile.

At supper we had fresh seal parts scooped from the communal washtub along with pinto beans and caribou jerky straight from the one-gallon pot, all of it washed down with Canadian whisky. Breakfast was coffee with eggs and the previous day's seal parts fried together, a mixture that included bacon until that ran out. I started pouring Canadian Club into my morning coffee to get past the overpowering taste of seal grease, although nothing could really kill it.

Those nights I lay among the harsh stones and tried to think why I was here or anywhere else—not an original question. The answer, formless and maddening as a splinter under the skin, was always nearby, or seemed so. Its impish laugh echoed all around. Whatever it might have been she was always part of it—a gossamer vision with long legs and a white smile who would treasure my every utterance and fuck me crippled. We'd awaken each day in a field of flowers, suffocated by the perfumed earth, washed in soft light refracted through mist. I knew the place well. It was very different from this place, or perhaps exactly like it. She's the only woman who ever broke my heart.

I wriggled deeper among the stones. When would she appear and lead me home by the hand? I felt her sudden warmth without evidence of sensation, saw the sea beside me sucked into the sky. Where was she, that perfect woman who would touch my face and tell me I was the one flagrant god in a false universe?

I've seen her many times at many locations, distantly, always with someone else. Either that or alone and waiting for him. Glimpses, nothing more. One time it was a subway platform seconds before she stepped into a train car, another time a dock where she waited anxiously for a commuter ferry, smiling when the vessel appeared as a silhouette suspended against the molten sunset.

I saw her again in Churchill late one December, the only time I visited when whaling was not the objective. The sun was a low circling orb filed small and dim by boreal winter and it felt as if daylight had departed forever. I was having coffee in the village's only diner. Fluorescent light ricocheted coldly off yellowed linoleum. Cheap plastic chairs scraped the floor. Cigarette smoke curled sinuously past windows wet with condensation, up the dirty walls to caress the stuffed heads of caribou. Outside, the parking lot was filled with idling pickups and snow machines abandoned haphazardly. At thirty below you don't risk shutting off your engine.

She was Inuit and came through the door laughing, accompanied by several young Inuit men. They took a table across the room, shedding hooded goose-down jackets and barking a confidence bestowed only on those with possession of place. She pulled off her helmet and shook out long black hair before glancing around, flashing even white teeth that had never chewed a sealskin mukluk and likely never would. The group ordered coffee, conversed loudly in Inuktitut, and was gone in a surge of frozen wind.

# *Delude, Memory!*

DON DELILLO WROTE IN *The Body Artist* that past, present, and future are not amenities of language. Actually, the opposite is true. In a complete description of the universe, time is not necessarily unidirectional, as intuition claims. From a third-person perspective the present does not exist in the physical world, nor do past and future. No equations describe the conceptual "now." Time is a simulacrum embedded in a self-made phenomenal experience, itself a shifting hallucination. Reality? A delusional representation of nature, a private rabbit hole of vanishingly small diameter within which we independently experience the limited world revealed to us. We take comfort in thinking that family and friends share this metaphorical space, an impossibility considering everyone's delusion is unique.

Our lonely tunnels are virtual holes drilled through the natural world, their walls lined with a thin layer of consciousness in which our illusion of "now"—that is, life in the first person—exists. These walls are permeable to the outside, although sensory input is severely restricted. Our minds occlude far more than they ever let in. For example, we can perceive only a narrow section of the electromagnetic spectrum. That golden sunset before you is a collaborative illusion created by your eyes and brain. The true reality outside human perception is colorless.

Each of us, we believe fervently, is the embodiment of throbbing tissue, emotions, memory. As proof, we cite existence in the first person: I am somebody; I'm *myself.* Sadly, the unconditional acceptance of this state known as naïve realism merely stretches the boundaries of the selfhood delusion. In truth, no such entity as a "self" exists. The reality available to us is entirely of our own construction, an unoccupied dwelling of endless labyrinths. Each human life is a play without an actor. Personal experiences occur in the absence of anyone to experience them; our thoughts have no thinkers. Unaware of the irony, we invent deities and worship them believing they exist in a virtual space apart from us, when in truth the stranger you're banging shoulders with on the subway is as distant as any god.

In his beautiful novel *In a Strange Room,* Damon Galgut wrote, "Things happen only once and are never repeated, never return. Except in memory." But how reliable is memory when reality itself is a construct? Which part of a recalled experience can be resurrected as even a ghost of the delusional "now" and how much is imagination filling in the blank spaces? The separation between memoir and fiction is less distinct than many imagine.

A thoughtful memoirist acknowledges this, if sometimes cryptically, and proceeds without regret. Joseph Mitchell in *Up in the Old Hotel* wrote, "I wanted these stories to be truthful rather than factual, but they are solidly based on facts." From Gabriel García Márquez's *Memories of My Melancholy Whores* came, "My only explanation is that just as real events are forgotten, some that never were can be in our memories as if they had happened." And André Malraux in *La Condition Humaine* advised us, *"Ce n'était ni vrai ni faux, c'était vécu."* (It was neither true nor false, but what was experienced.) When writing this book I chose as my guide Jean Baudrillard, who said in *Simulacra and Simulation*, "When the real is no longer what it was, nostalgia assumes its full meaning." This seems entirely consistent with Thomas Metzinger's superb synthesis of philosophy and neuroscience titled *Being No One*.

The stories I've presented are true, but like all memories they drifted across my consciousness as fragments often displaced out of time. Any chronology is unavoidably artifactual in this sense. Similar to the illusion of time passing, recounting a life presents the illusion of gliding sequentially from past to present. But that's part of humankind's naïve realism as conceived by Metzinger's phenomenal self-model, a view of the world so perfectly transparent that despite being virtual it appears real to us.

Rarely, you encounter someone who understands this at some level; that is, how the conceptual "now" is an impossibility because the present is already the past and the future never arrives. There was a bar owner in the town where I enrolled as a college freshman. A couple of days before classes started he placed a sign in his window saying Free Beer Tomorrow. The next afternoon I was part of a long line of expectant freshmen waiting for the door to open. That's when the owner stepped outside and asked if we were wanting free beer. Yes, we told him. "Well," he said, "read the goddamn sign. It says Free Beer *Tomorrow.* Now if you feel like *buying* beer *today,* come on in." We did, of course. He pulled this ruse for the benefit of freshmen every autumn, and it never failed.

West Virginia's rural culture in the forties and fifties was utilitarian. Nature was to be used, just as the Bible advised. It was put here by God to serve humankind, so in all innocence the land was logged, the streams polluted, the wildlife shot. Little consideration was given to conserving resources that everyone understood would be around forever. Anyway, in times of dire need God would always provide, never mind Old Testament tales of pestilence and famine and our modern world's recent encounter with the Holocaust.

All the kids had pets. These existed apart from other animals, which occupied such categories as vermin, game, spectacle, and domestically-raised food. Animals needed a purpose to justify their existence; if not, they were killed or simply ignored. An incident at the Howards' farm provides an example. It involved a dog from the resident mutt pack. The dog was a few months old with short brown hair, his heritage mostly hound. By any account he was an ordinary, nameless dog. Mr. H was training him to trail rabbits, but he was gun-shy and ran away yelping in fear when anyone discharged a firearm nearby.

One fall morning Mr. H decided this was unacceptable. He got a shotgun and a length of rope and went into the woods with Dewey, Millard, and me trailing along. We figured it was a training session. The dog was ecstatic, bounding ahead and stopping now and then to sniff the ground, until Mr. H tied him to a tree and told us to step away. The dog seemed confused and tried to return to us only to be yanked back by the rope. He whined and panted. He pranced coquettishly back and forth at his limits of restraint, then crouched with chin between his paws and tail in the air soliciting us to approach and play, and Mr. H shot him dead. "I won't feed a useless dog," he said. That would never have happened if a pet failed to meet expectations, as the next example shows.

At some point around this time I announced that I wanted a dog of my own. The Howards said I could have Butchie, one of their pack, so I took him home. Butchie was a black mutt of medium size and no obvious parentage, but Daddy figured any dog could be trained to flush rabbits out of the briers, hound or not. I was to be the trainer. I went down to the hard road and found a car-struck rabbit still reasonably fresh. I tied it to a string and got Butchie to follow along as I dragged it behind me. He liked the game so much it was hard keeping the rabbit out of his mouth. I showed Daddy how adept Butchie was at carrying rabbits around.

That Saturday we set out through the fields, Daddy carrying the .410 shotgun. We walked until coming on a large patch of greenbriers. "There's probably rabbits in there," Daddy said. "Tell the dog to flush them out so I can get a clear shot." I gave Butchie the command, and he dived in. We heard lots of thrashing around and saw the bushes moving. Then Butchie appeared suddenly with a live adult rabbit in his mouth, which he brought over and dropped at our feet. The rabbit sat up unharmed, confused, and soaked with dog spit.

Daddy looked down at it. "Well I'll be goddamned," he said. "This isn't what I expected." We left the rabbit to celebrate its good fortune and the three of us walked home.

Events should be interpreted in the context of history and culture, and this obviously includes how we think of nature. The developed world has become ever more sensitized to the plight of animals. Today, even the killing of sharks for their fins or for sport is frowned on by many, and rightly so. Those who take a dim view of my past participation in live-capturing whales and shooting seals need to consider that only a few years previously a commercial whaling station operated in Churchill, Manitoba, and that the subsistence hunting of seals was then—and is today—part of Inuit culture.

Rest assured, my experiences recounted here will never be reprised. A zoo or public aquarium could, in those days, apply for permits to catch dolphins and whales for public display, but today no government agency in the US or Canada would grant approval. Nor is there any good reason for doing so. I've made the argument why exhibiting live animals is anachronistic in the postmodern age as the technologies of film and virtual reality in many guises bring us ever closer to mimicking the phenomenal self-model constructed by our own brains. We understand them at an intimate level of consciousness no aquarium or zoo exhibit can match. Observing a snoozing lion in a cage is a poor facsimile of a wild lion, and nobody is fooled.

But back to the water. Jean-Paul Sartre wrote in *Nausea,* "The *true* [Sartre's emphasis] sea is cold and black, full of animals; it crawls under this thin green film made to deceive human beings." My perception is the opposite. To me the emergent world is a noisy, unpleasant place overflowing with deceit. I mistrusted it as a child and still do. Underwater, the silence lets me speak inside myself, and I can hear secret things. And you up there, the remainder of humanity, you might too if you put aside the aimless gestures, the nattering, the disposable conversations, the notion you're special and the world actually cares. That's why I have nothing else to say on the matter. Not now, not ever.

## *About Stephen Spotte*

Stephen Spotte, a marine scientist, was born and raised in West Virginia. He has been a field biologist for the US Army Corps of Engineers (Waterways Experiment Station, Vicksburg, Mississippi); curator and later director of Aquarium of Niagara Falls (New York); curator of the New York Aquarium and Osborn Laboratories of Marine Science (Brooklyn, New York); director of Mystic Aquarium (Mystic, Connecticut); executive director of Sea Research Foundation and research scientist at the Marine Sciences and Technology Center, University of Connecticut (Groton, Connecticut); principal investigator, Coral Reef Ecology Program (Turks and Caicos Islands, BWI), and adjunct scientist at Mote Marine Laboratory (Sarasota, Florida). Dr. Spotte has a B.S. degree from Marshall University, a PhD from the University of Southern Mississippi, and is author or coauthor of more than eighty scientific papers on marine biology, ocean chemistry and engineering, and aquaculture. Field research has encompassed the Canadian Arctic, Bering Sea, West Indies, Indo-West Pacific, Central America, and the Amazon basin of Ecuador and Brazil. His popular articles about the sea have appeared in *National Wildlife, On the Sound, Animal Kingdom, Explorers Journal*, and *Science Digest.* Dr. Spotte has published eighteen books, including three volumes of fiction, a memoir, and a work of cultural theory. He also holds a US Merchant Marine officer's license.